Praise for The Presentation Workout

'Absolutely perfect – full of hints and tips for every type of presentation; especially useful for those with little or no experience and a great refresher for anyone wanting to polish their skills and make their presentations even more memorable.'

Louise Bateman, Human Resources Director,
Royal Masonic Benevolent Institution

'Presenting effectively has become a fundamental "must have" for most senior executives and Kate Atkin brilliantly captures the tips, tools, strategies and techniques of how to become an accomplished presenter. A great read and it's a book that I will be continually referring to!'

Andrew Richards, Group Managing Director, Linden Homes

'Novices and practicing presenters alike will find a range of hints and tips here to build on existing skills whatever the purpose or the medium for their key messages. Easy to read and dip into as a lasting reference tool.'

Lee Mortimer, Training Quality Manager, Capita Learning Services

The Presentation Workout

The Presentation Workout

The 10 tried-and-tested steps that will build your presenting skills

Kate Atkin

PEARSON

Harlow, England • London • New York • Boston • San Francisco • Toronto • Sydney
Auckland • Singapore • Hong Kong • Tokyo • Seoul • Taipei • New Delhi
Cape Town • São Paulo • Mexico City • Madrid • Amsterdam • Munich • Paris • Milan

Pearson Education Limited
Edinburgh Gate
Harlow CM20 2JE
United Kingdom
Tel: +44 (0)1279 623623
Web: www.pearson.com/uk

First published 2015 (print and electronic)

© Pearson Education Limited 2015 (print and electronic)

The right of Kate Atkin to be identified as author of this work has been asserted by her in accordance with the Copyright, Designs and Patents Act 1988.

Pearson Education is not responsible for the content of third-party internet sites.

The screenshots in this book are reprinted by permission of Microsoft Corporation.

ISBN: 978-1-292-07669-0 (print)
     978-1-292-07671-3 (PDF)
     978-1-292-07672-0 (ePub)
     978-1-292-07670-6 (eText)

British Library Cataloguing-in-Publication Data
A catalogue record for the print edition is available from the British Library

Library of Congress Cataloging-in-Publication Data
Atkin, Kate.
  The presentation workout : the 10 tried-and-tested steps that will build your
    presenting skills / Kate Atkin. pages cm
  Includes bibliographical references.
  ISBN 978-1-292-07669-0
  1. Business presentations. 2. Communication in management. I. Title.
  HF5718.22.A865 2015
  658.4'52–dc23

                         2015019869

10 9 8 7 6 5 4 3 2 1
19 18 17 16 15

Cover design by Two Associates
Print edition typeset in 10/13 Scene Std by 71
Print edition printed in Great Britain by Henry Ling Ltd, at the Dorset Press, Dorchester, Dorset

NOTE THAT ANY PAGE CROSS REFERENCES REFER TO THE PRINT EDITION

Contents

Decide whether a presentation is the best way to get your message across. Identify the purpose of your presentation; whether it is tell, sell, impel or entertain. Recognise your desired results and consider whether an alternative to a presentation could get your message across more effectively.

Examine your audience; who are they, what are they looking for, why should they listen to you? Generate rapport and create empathy with your audience, both before your presentation and during.

Begin designing and writing your presentation. Add structure to your message. Discover the 'power of three', use repetition wisely and create verbal signposts.

Contents

Contents

About the author

Kate Atkin is an inspirational speaker, facilitator and author on presentation skills. Recognised as the Most Outstanding Trainer in JCI UK, Kate is also a World Debating Champion, number one Speech Evaluator in the UK and Ireland (2007) with Toastmasters International and European runner up in the JCI Public Speaking competition.

A fellow of the Professional Speaking Association, member of the Chartered Institute for Personnel and Development and the Association for Coaching, Kate is also an associate of the Chartered Institute of Bankers and a Senator of Junior Chamber International.

Kate holds a Master of Applied Positive Psychology degree and is a regular speaker on the mindset needed to generate flourishing and confidence. She works with companies and individuals who wish to bring about positive change.

Find out more about Kate at: **www.kateatkin.com**

Author's acknowledgements

With particular thanks to all who contributed to the writing of this book, not just those who contributed their words directly, but also to all my clients who have added something to my knowledge and experience. Also a big thank you to my husband Stuart Jessup for his patience, support and backing.

Thanks must also go to my father, Bill Atkin, who gave me his guidance and encouragement in my teenage years when I first started making presentations.

Publisher's acknowledgements

Picture credits

The publisher would like to thank the following for their kind permission to reproduce their photographs:

Alamy Images: PEOPLESTOCK page 15, AF archive page 21, JCM Images page 26, dpa picture alliance page 47, Tony Tallec page 132; **Getty Images:** Beth Hall / Bloomberg page 9, David Paul Morris page 29, Keystone page 31, Frank Capri / Hulton Archive page 40, JOHN G. MABANGLO / AFP page 64; **Shutterstock.com:** Andrey_Popov page 6, Richard Peterson page 10, wavebreakmedia page 19, Lee Yiu Tung page 32, Ramon Espelt Photography page 55, bikeriderlondon pages 61 and 142, Rawpixel page 44, Maxim Blinkov page 68, Stuart Jenner page 88, Gruffi page 118, Hayati Kayhan page 120, wavebreakmedia page 160.

Cartoons:

Randy Glasbergen: page 183, ©Randy Glasbergen, www.glasbergen.com

All other images © Pearson Education

Every effort has been made to trace the copyright holders and we apologise in advance for any unintentional omissions. We would be pleased to insert the appropriate acknowledgement in any subsequent edition of this publication.

Introduction

Oh no ... I've got to give a presentation; I hate giving presentations.

Have you ever had a thought like that?

So many of us need to give presentations – not necessarily a formal 45-minute talk from a stage but often a short 5-minute convincer in a meeting, an update on your work on a regular basis or a sales pitch to a prospective customer. The business world today also demands more online presentations, webinars and video conferencing.

Yet having to give a presentation can strike dread into the heart of many and has been said to be feared more than death itself; though that is a rather extreme reaction to the thought of standing up in front of a group of people.

Who is this book for?

If you need to give presentations, in whatever form, this book is for you.

But can presentation skills be learned from a book?

First of all, you really do need to take every opportunity to stand on your feet in front of people to increase your skills as a presenter. But, whatever type of presentation you are giving, there are ground rules that will make every one of your presentations more effective and there are many tips, tools and techniques that you can learn in advance. These are covered in this book, together with exercises to help you increase your knowledge and skills.

Most of the references are for face-to-face presentations, but you can adapt the ideas for both online webinars and video conferences, and there are some specific tips relating to those in **Part 2**.

The aim of this book is to offer something for everyone, from the nervous, novice presenter through to tips to tweak and polish confident performances.

In my many years of experience in training people in presentation skills, workshop participants tend to fall into one of four categories:

High confidence Low(ish) ability	High confidence High ability
Thought they were good presenters, but have been told that their skills need to be improved	Seeking a tip to make a 1% difference to effective presentations
Low confidence Low ability	**Low confidence High ability**
Novice presenters looking for techniques and tips, especially on how to handle nerves	Wanting ways to boost their self-confidence before making presentations

My guess is that you as a reader will recognise yourself as fitting into one of those categories.

Whatever the type of presentation you are giving, to whatever audience, there is always something that will make your communication even more effective. Read this book with that in mind and it will help you to give your next presentation the extra polish that it deserves.

Ready to learn?

You will get the greatest benefit from this book by practising as well as reading.

As Aristotle once said:

> *For the things we have to learn before we can do them, we learn by doing them.*

To assist you in learning the art of making effective presentations you will be encouraged to take time out from reading to create your own presentation, practise a concept and pay a visit to the online content, where you will find video examples, interviews and blog posts.

I will be using a few icons in this book to guide you to the relevant activities. These are:

Activity   **Key idea**   **Media**

The book starts with 10 'how to . . .' steps. These provide you with the knowledge that an effective presenter needs. Inside each step you will find exercises and checklists to help embed your learning and encourage you to incorporate it into your next presentation. These steps do not have to be completed in order; depending on your knowledge and the type of presentation you are preparing for, you may find that some steps are more relevant than others.

Next, the 10 skills, in **Part 2**, cover how to use this knowledge in action by examining some of the different situations in which you may be required to give a presentation. You will then find 10 challenges in **Part 3**, covering some common presentation challenges that you may face – for instance, how to manage your nerves. Finally, the 'putting it into action' section provides you with a guide to using your skills in action, in conjunction with a mentor, to enable you to really embed your learning and gather useful feedback on your progress.

In addition, there is a pre- and post- self-assessment questionnaire to help you assess your progress. It is a little like going to the gym and calibrating your heart rate, blood pressure and BMI at the start of your exercise regime and then again in 6 months.

You might not see big changes at the beginning, but if you keep going, one idea at a time, you will see a cumulative effect.

I have had the pleasure over many years of not only training people in presentation skills, but in making countless presentations myself, both for work and competitively (yes, just for fun!). I continue to learn each time I make a presentation, and I hope this book encourages you to take your own presentations to the next level, wherever that might be.

Self-assessment questionnaire

Use the following questionnaire to calibrate your current presentation skills. You will be able to assess which areas you enjoy when giving presentations, what gives you energy and whether you need to find a way to do certain things more often.

Score yourself on a scale of 1 to 10, with 10 indicating a high level of confidence and skill and 1 the lowest.

1. I feel energised by speaking to people.

2. I rarely suffer from nerves when speaking in public.

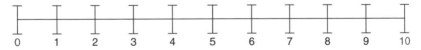

3. I find it easy to express my thoughts.

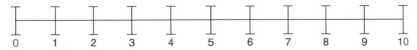

4. I find it easy to speak up in meetings.

5. I like crafting words to express myself.

6. I enjoy being the centre of attention.

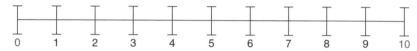

7. I am confident in my use of PowerPoint.

8. I find it easy to make persuasive presentations.

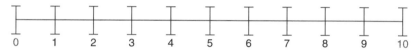

9. I use my body and gestures effectively when communicating to others.

10. I frequently take up opportunities to present to people.

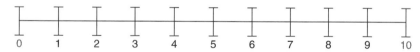

Add up your scores to give you an idea of how comfortable and confident you feel about making presentations at the moment, on a scale of 0 to 100.

If your score is between 80 and 100 you're very confident at giving presentations and enjoy the limelight. However, be aware that overconfidence might creep in and you could perhaps prepare your presentations a little more, rather than 'wing' them.

If your score is between 50 and 80 then there is some room to improve your confidence and ability when presenting, but you probably already know a fair amount.

If your score is below 50 you are likely to need a confidence boost, as well as improved skills. You might like to start by reading **Step 9** on confidence and then return to **Step 1**.

Keep in mind that this is your opinion; you might like to ask your manager, mentor or colleagues to score you as well, to gather different views.

As you work your way through the book, you will find that some of the answers you gave change as you understand more about presenting successfully. For example, use of body language and gestures (Question 9) are covered in **Steps 6** and **9**; after reading these you may choose to change the way you stand and move when presenting.

You are encouraged to retake the questionnaire after you have worked through the book in order to assess your progress, and at 6-monthly intervals as you continue to increase your skills.

So, ready to learn?

I hope you enjoy the process.

Kate

kate@kateatkin.com

Part 1

10 steps to present with style

Step 1

What is the purpose of your presentation?

After reading this step you will be able to:

- Decide whether a presentation is the right medium for your message
- Identify benefits and drawbacks of the alternatives to a presentation
- Understand the type of presentation you are giving.

While this book is about making presentations, the first thing to ask yourself is whether a presentation is actually the best way to get your message across. For many people, a presentation is the *default* way to get a message across, not necessarily the best.

It is often easier to put a bullet-point-style presentation together, go through the slides with the people you want to communicate with, pass them a hand-out of the slides and your job is done. Your staff, colleagues or clients have all the information they need to do whatever you have asked and, of course, they will get on with it.

However, the message rarely comes across that clearly and is rarely acted upon in the way you intended, particularly in the workplace. Many an assumption is made that a presentation will bring about the desired effect. While a slide presentation might be a quick way of disseminating information, it does not mean the information has been heard, or will be acted upon. Also, there are many disadvantages to using slides, and **Step 6** discusses these.

 A presentation is *one* way of communicating but not necessarily the *best* way.

So, before you plunge headlong into crafting your presentation, take a moment to read this step and consider your audience, your message and the reason you want to impart the information.

Only then can you decide whether a presentation is the best medium.

Before deciding whether or not to make a presentation, there are a number of questions it is useful to ask yourself to help identify the key components of your message:

- What do you want to say?
- Why do you want to say it?
- What is the purpose of putting your message across?
- What do you want your audience to do with your information?

- After listening to your information, what action or reaction are you seeking from your audience?
- Is there a better way of getting your information across?

I will now explore each of these in more detail.

What do you want to say?

Give some thought to your message; what do you really want to say?

For instance, is it to broadcast some information that is newsworthy to you, such as winning a new contract, a breakthrough on product design or an IT workaround you have just discovered?

In this case, check whether your message is also newsworthy to your audience. In today's world everyone is short of time, and giving up precious minutes to attend a meeting to listen to something that has no bearing on their way of working is going to be seen as a waste of time and may create resentment, possibly resulting in no one listening to your future presentations. However, if your information is a key part of the company's change-management process and will impact on your audience over the next few weeks then, if presented effectively, you are likely to have their attention.

If the information is complex, would a briefing note be a better option followed up with one-to-one meetings or small discussion groups? If the information is simple or a simple request, would a request in person or a phone call or email suffice?

Advances in technology have meant that presentations no longer have to be given to large groups in person, and telephone calls are no longer just one to one. Skype and Google Hangouts allow for video calls, or multiple users on a call at the same time, and they can be recorded for non-attendees to watch or listen to later. In addition, your company might have a conference call facility, possibly using a speaker phone or even a full-blown video conferencing suite.

These are all alternatives to giving a stand-up presentation to a group of people. However, the method you choose will depend on your information, the purpose of your presentation and also your audience.

Don't use technology just because it is available. Select what is most appropriate for your message.

Maybe a presentation wasn't quite the right choice

Why do you want to say it?

Telling someone how great you are at winning contracts might not be the best way of endearing yourself to colleagues. However, if you have just won a new piece of work and you need the support of others to fulfil the contract, then you have a reason to engage with your colleagues. Or perhaps you have found an influencing style that helped you win the contract and you want to share that with your sales colleagues.

Take some time to assess your own reasons for speaking, and give consideration to others' reasons for listening.

What is the purpose of putting your message across?

Be honest here: is it to brag about your accomplishments, or to really help others achieve? Save bragging about your own accomplishments for the coffee machine conversations and your appraisal. Equally, bragging about how great your company or your products are isn't going to win you many sales, unless you first take the time to find out whether your product or service solves the customer's problem.

What do you want your audience to do with your information?

If the answer to this question is 'nothing, I just wanted to tell them', think before you turn it into a presentation. There must be a reason why you want them to hear it. See the sections below on 'Tell', 'Sell', 'Impel' or 'Entertain' to help identify your reason.

If you are being asked to speak by someone else, check with them what they want the audience to think, feel and do as a result of listening to the presentation. Based on the answer, you will be able to identify which type of presentation you are being asked to give.

What actions or reactions are you seeking from your audience?

If you are seeking individual views on your information, then a group presentation is unlikely to provide an environment where everyone will speak up. You might be more effective having one-to-one discussions. Are you expecting any hostility or resistance? If so, how will you deal with this in a large group? (See **Step 2**: Understand your audience and connect with them.) How will you gauge people's reactions to your information?

Is there a better way of getting your information across?

There are benefits and drawbacks to all methods of communication, but before you decide to give a presentation consider whether an alternative method might be more effective in getting your message across. Other options might include using a round-table format rather than a staged presentation, making telephone or video-conferencing calls or providing a written brief.

If you do conclude that a presentation is the best way of getting your information across, then the next step is to look at your message.

Sadly there are many presentations that end up full of waffle, without a clear purpose, message or call to action and without audience engagement. If you take some time at the start of your preparation to think about the purpose of your message, you are well on your way to avoiding these pitfalls.

 What is the purpose of your presentation: to tell, sell, impel or entertain?

Tell

Your presentation is to inform, but doesn't require any action.

The tell presentation is a way of broadcasting your message to a large group of people. It could be viewed as standing in the street shouting through a megaphone. Everyone hears the same message, at the same time. Hopefully your audience will be paying a little more attention than they would to the town crier.

One thing to keep in mind with broadcast and tell presentations is that while the same information reaches everybody's ears at the same time, it is very difficult to verify they have heard what you meant. Everybody has their individual filters and biases and will interpret information slightly differently.

The tell method is often used by companies to broadcast a corporate message. This can be internally to staff, externally to shareholders or at a press briefing. Team briefings, Monday-morning updates and huddles are other uses of the tell presentation.

Sell

The sell presentation is the staple of sales professionals. But there are many more circumstances in which this type of presentation is required. These could be to convince senior managers about an idea for a new project or a project revision, to gain buy-in to a new way of working or to inform and sell a new management structure to staff.

Whatever the purpose of your sell presentation, you will need to ensure there is a call to action at the end to establish buy-in, a purchase or the next step along the way to the 'sale'.

Impel

When a presentation is made with the intent to encourage people into a course of action it is an impel presentation. Motivational or inspirational presentations are probably the most common type of impel presentations. The idea is to encourage a new way of thinking, release more creativity or create renewed enthusiasm within the audience.

Walmart delivers a tell presentation at its annual employees and shareholders meeting

There are motivational speakers who whip up their audiences into a fervour, then ask a series of questions to get 'yes' answers (such as would you like to earn more money, be more successful, have more holidays), before getting people to sign up to their programmes. It sways some people, but the cynic in me worries about the ethics of persuading people to commit 'in the heat of the moment'. In any case, this impel style only suits a certain type of presenter; if it matches your values, by all means go ahead. However, you may decide to persuade your audience with a quieter form of the motivational impel. There is more about how to do this in **Parts 2 and 3**.

 See videos demonstrating the different presentation styles at: www.thebusinessgym.net

Entertain

The entertainment speech is unlikely to be delivered during the working day.

You might find the entertain style in use at the theatre or in stand-up comedy. In a business context it occurs most often in an after-dinner speech. Be warned though, after dinner an audience may be less inclined to listen or to be polite if they don't like the speech. An entertainment speech needs to be fast paced to keep the attention of the audience and is usually humorous.

No need to go this far in your efforts to entertain

Case study

Here are a few tips on entertainment speeches from John Hotowka, a former magician who uses magic and comedy to create business messages through entertainment. Known as the 'Laughter Dinner Speaker', John is often called upon to round off events in a memorable and humorous way.

I started my career in 1989 as a magician performing magic and comedy after dinner; I still do from time to time. There's no business message it's just fun and laugh out loud entertainment. The purpose is to finish the night on a high with some fun and make the event memorable. If the audience all know each other I do my homework before the event and do my best to include appropriate satirical humour about the industry and company as well as various characters within the group. If the audience do not know each other 'inside jokes' just won't work, in that case I do my best to find something they have in common that they can laugh about and bond.

I believe all speakers should be entertaining particularly after dinner and by entertaining I don't mean funny. The speaker needs to have presence and hold the audience's attention as once a belly full of food and alcohol have been consumed attention can quickly wane. Comedy and great story-telling skills helps hold attention.

Ideally tell stories about situations your audience can identify with, think along the lines of observational comedy. Audiences are always interested in challenges you've faced that are similar to their challenges and insights on how to deal with them is always appreciated. Self-deprecating humour works well too.

Regarding business speaking I believe a good rule of thumb to be as follows: for daytime events a presentation should be 80% content and 20% entertainment and for after dinner 20% content and 80% entertainment.

 **Exercise**

Think about your next presentation; take a moment to write down its purpose.

Now reread the purpose and ask yourself whether a presentation is the most effective way of getting your message across. Would an alternative be as effective, or more effective?

If a presentation is the most effective way, identify whether it needs to be in a tell, sell, impel or entertain style.

Call to action

- What alternative methods are there other than a presentation?

- Is a presentation the best way to get your message across?

- What type of presentation are you giving: tell, sell, impel or entertain?

- What do you want the audience to do after your presentation?

Step 2

Understand your audience and connect with them

After reading this step you will be able to:

- Profile your audience – who are they, what are their interests and what might they want from your presentation?
- Make a connection and build rapport
- Keep the attention and interest of your audience.

Having decided that a presentation is the best method of getting your information across, and identified whether you will be using a tell, sell, impel or entertain style, it is now time to take a look at your audience. A common mistake when preparing a presentation is to start by preparing in detail the message you want to get across. Before you do that, take a step back and give some consideration to your audience. This step will take you through that process.

Who are your audience?

Before you begin crafting your message, take time to go through the following questions. They will help you to look at what you want to say from the audience's point of view.

What is their background?

What mood will they be in?

What age range are they?

How culturally diverse will they be?

How many will there be?

What job(s) do they do?

What is the hierarchy and is it important to their culture?

Will the boss be present?

How will that affect the mood?

What are they interested in?

What problems do they have?

What are their current challenges?

What could their objections be to your message?

Who is likely to be in favour?

 And possibly the biggest question: why should they listen to you?

And you thought I was actually listening to what you were saying...

Identifying with your audience

- Poor presenters will craft their message and deliver it, despite any reaction from the audience.
- A good presenter will take the audience into account when crafting the message.
- An excellent presenter will be able to consider the audience in advance, but also respond to their reactions while delivering the presentation itself.

Creating a connection and generating empathy and rapport with your audience means they are more likely to listen to your message. That doesn't mean they will necessarily agree with you, but it does at least give you a chance of being heard.

There are a few steps that can help you identify with your audience and create rapport from the outset. If you are not the organiser, and if you don't know your audience, why not ask the person organising the event for the names and contact details of a few people who will be there and ask if you can contact them ahead of time? If you are giving a presentation to your work colleagues the same tips apply, but you will already have their contact details.

Once you make contact, preferably by phone or in person rather than email as that way you can gauge their reaction, you can ask a few of the questions listed above to find out what their issues are, what they want to know from you and what their objections or questions might be.

Not only will this give you valuable information to include in your presentation, it will provide you with a few people you already know, and who already know you. On the day they are likely to be friendly faces in the audience, and you will be seen as someone who takes the trouble to prepare thoroughly. It will also provide a few people for you to meet in person as soon as you arrive, which can help to calm any nerves you may have.

However, if you don't get enough notice of your presentation to speak to some audience members in advance, ensure you get there early enough on the day to do so. If it is a meeting, turn up in time to have a short chat with those who also arrive early. This can even be done in online, virtual presentations, when the presenter has signed in to the call early and takes the opportunity to talk to people as they sign in.

If it is a big conference you are presenting at it may be possible and applicable to record a short video of you talking directly to an audience, which is made available online to watch before the event. Another technique that can be used to make a connection beforehand is an online survey. This can help to gather information on the issues being faced, find out questions in advance or establish the audience's interests. Technology is providing ever-changing ways to connect with people, but in my view there is still no substitute for talking face to face.

Creating rapport

There is a lot to be said for having the audience on your side before you start, but that is not always possible, even if you do know them in advance. Sometimes your message might be controversial, or one that will stir up past resentments. If you can, consult widely before you make your presentation; find out where the assent and dissent is likely to come from so you know who is on your side.

The Japanese have a name for this method of influencing: *nemawashi*. *Nemawashi*, literally 'going around the roots', originally referred to transplanting trees, such as in the art of bonsai. It also refers to a method of gathering information in advance of a meeting to see who is for and who is against a proposal, and is particularly useful when relating to proposed changes. Depending on the culture of the organisation you are working in, this may work well. However, be aware of the tendency for office gossip, as people may wonder what the individual meetings are all about if you are not able to be open, resulting in Chinese whispers and mixed messages.

Rapport should also be established on the day of your presentation. Gather a few comments when talking to people beforehand, and make a reference to them during your talk using a phrase such as: 'From comments I heard earlier some of you believe X while others believe Y.' Or put yourself in your audience's mindset and verbally guess what they might be thinking by making a statement such as: 'I guess some of you may be thinking. . . .'

Rapport is also made through handshakes, eye contact and body language. It is important to focus outwards; a nervous presenter often finds it difficult to create rapport because they are worried about what other people think. You can find some tips on handling nerves in **Part 3**.

Age profile

The age range of your audience will have an impact on several aspects of your presentation.

Consider the formality of the language: what is appropriate? Will they be used to slang or understand your jargon or your TLAs (three-letter acronyms)?

How attentive are they likely to be? It is often assumed that an audience with an older profile will be more attentive, but this may just be that they have learned to be polite and hide their boredom. Younger audiences definitely need a faster pace, anecdotes and possibly videos embedded in your slides to keep them interested.

However, why should older audiences be denied that engagement?

 Consider your audience profile, but ensure you don't make assumptions.

Use vulnerability or humour to generate rapport

Adam Grant in his book *Give and Take* talks about the value of vulnerability. He cites a course he gave to a group of senior military leaders when he was 26. The audience were twice his age and although Grant had qualifications and knowledge of his topic, the feedback demonstrated that the age differential was a barrier to them learning the lessons he was trying to put across. So the second time Grant gave the same course he started with a different opening, acknowledging the audience's likely objection about his age: 'I know what you're thinking right now: what can I possibly learn from a professor who's 12 years old?' The second course was far more successful.

David Hyner, a UK speaker on achieving MASSIVE goals, opens his talks with the line: 'I know what you're thinking . . . OH NO . . . it's a little fat guy from Birmingham with a really weird haircut!'

Both of these examples show self-deprecating humour towards the speaker themselves, not their content or the audience. Addressing the audience's concerns at the start can open up their hearts and minds to listen to your content.

Laughter is also a great way to generate rapport.

I once opened up a presentation using a quote from Einstein – 'reality is an illusion, albeit a rather persistent one' – and then questioned whether the business issues the audience were facing were real or illusory. I went on to observe that I was the only woman in the room and that was definitely reality, not an illusion. It brought a laugh from everyone and helped to break the ice.

The audience is engaged

Demonstrating empathy

At the time of writing this section, the debate on the vote regarding Scottish independence was raging with just two days to go. David Cameron had just made an emotional appeal to the Scots to stay in the Union, saying that he would be 'utterly heartbroken' if Scotland voted for independence. But this is all about David Cameron's emotions, not the emotions of the Scots. That is not a great demonstration of empathy.

When demonstrating empathy, the worst thing you can do is use the phrase 'I understand how you feel'. The second worst thing is to recount a similar situation you were once in. Neither demonstrates empathy; nor does stating your own emotions.

Empathy, as defined in the Oxford Dictionary,[1] is 'the ability to understand and share the feelings of another'. To understand another person's feelings requires questions to be asked and listening to take place, but doing this individually with a large group is impossible. To create empathy with large groups requires a little guess-work. If you use the language of suggestion to guess

[1] www.oxforddictionaries.com/definition/english/empathy

how your audience might be feeling, it will come across that you care, have given their feelings some thought and taken them into account as people, not just an audience mass.

Depending on the scenario, you might like to use some of the following words and phrases:

- 'At this point I guess some of you may be feeling some of these emotions . . . (for example: frustration, confusion, worry, concern, excitement, interest, pride, relief).'
- 'Right now you might be thinking . . .'
- '. . . here we go again . . . what's different this time . . . this sounds a great opportunity . . . how does this apply to me.'

 View videos showing how to generate rapport and create empathy at:

www.thebusinessgym.net

Case study

I once gave a keynote speech to a Young Enterprise awards ceremony and arrived in time to go around the contestants' business stands, speak to the young people and listen to their own presentations before giving mine. The chairperson of the awards remarked on this and said not many keynote speakers arrive in time to hear the contestants' presentations or speak to them beforehand. Doing so meant I could tailor my presentation to include a few references to the teams and their businesses and make it very relevant for the audience.

I have also attended a presentation where the audience of about 30 people were gathering in a small room and the presenter sat behind his desk looking through his notes and studiously avoiding eye contact with anyone until it was time for him to start speaking. Although he gave a very informative presentation he didn't get much reaction from the audience or many questions at the end. I wonder whether it was to do with the lack of connection made at the start.

Arriving early is something I do as a matter of course, but it is surprising how many people don't give themselves this extra time to connect with the audience. It is about the audience, not about the presenter.

'But enough about me, let's talk about you . . . what do you think about me?' CC Bloom, played by Bette Midler in *Beaches*, 1988

 Exercise

For your next presentation, take 5 minutes to go through these questions and identify the issues from your audience's point of view.

- What is their background?
- What mood will they be in?
- What age range are they?
- How culturally diverse will they be?
- How many will there be?
- What job(s) do they do?
- What is the hierarchy and is it important to their culture?

- Will the boss be present?
- How will that affect the mood?
- What are they interested in?
- What problems do they have?
- What are their current challenges?
- What could their objections be to your message?
- Who is likely to be in favour?

 And, as before, why should they listen to you?

Then jot down the message(s) you want to get across.

Identify any discrepancies or potential areas of conflict, as well as those with similarities.

For any identified discrepancies or areas of potential conflict, include them in your presentation so you are the first to raise them. For instance, if your audience are expecting some new procedures to be put in place that will take extra time, you could make a statement to the effect of: 'Well, I guess you're all expecting the new procedures to take extra time, and you'd be right. So why are we changing things and where will the benefits be found?'

Then address those questions in your presentation.

Call to action

- Assess your audience:
  - o What do they want to know?
  - o What are their challenges?
  - o What might their objections be?
- Connect with your audience before your presentation.
- Design your presentation with your audience in mind, not just your message.

Step 3

Structure your presentation and craft your words

After reading this step you will be able to:

- Begin writing your presentation
- Practise using the power of three
- Get yourself out of the way (it's about your audience, not about you).

Do not say a little in many words but a great deal in a few.

Pythagoras

There are many ways to begin crafting the words you would like to say in your presentation. One way is to begin by writing your message out word for word, which works for some people. In this step I will offer a couple of alternatives that might help those of you who do not have a fully formed presentation in your head, and will enable those of you who do to make your presentation more fluid. This step will also provide you with guidance and exercises to practise using the power of three, and when it might be appropriate to use 'we' rather than 'I' as you speak.

Structuring your presentation

When designing the structure of your presentation remember to keep the audience in mind, as discussed in the previous step.

A good presentation has structure, regardless of whether it is carefully crafted word for word, or put together 'on the fly'. A structure, even one as simple as a beginning, middle and end, can be surprisingly effective.

How many times have you heard someone launch into a full and detailed explanation without any set-up? Has it left you wondering about the background to the issue, why they are telling you the information or when they might draw to an end?

Or have you ever listened to a presentation that came to an apparent abrupt conclusion and you were left wondering what to do with the information you had just heard, who is responsible for taking action and what were they really asking?

These pitfalls can be avoided by remembering to give your presentation three basic elements: a beginning, middle and end.

Beginning

The start of your presentation sets the tone for what is to come. Your set-up could be based on intrigue, a fact, statement or background detail. See the INTRO section in **Step 4** for more detail.

Middle

This is where you will have the bulk of your information, facts, figures and persuasive argument if necessary. The structure section below will help you to craft it.

End

Make sure your presentation has a close. Include a call to action, recap your opening, or close with a rallying cry. See **Step 10** for more detail on how to close your presentation.

Ways to create structure

Let's take a look at a couple of ways to help organise your presentation, bring out your ideas and create some structure.

The Post-it approach

I was introduced to this method by Betty Cooper, an expert coach to professional speakers, based in Canada. Since then I have used it to good effect and it may work for you. You will need a number of different-sized Post-its, from the smallest, just bigger than a postage stamp, to the really large ones on which you can write a few sentences.

The idea is to create your key message(s) on the largest Post-its and use progressively smaller Post-its for sub-messages. Then use additional Post-its for the stories that illustrate your message. You can build a bank of stories, placing one Post-it on top of the other, which allows you to review and select the most appropriate or even to choose to have three stories to illustrate one message.

The advantage of using Post-its is that you can create as many points and stories as you wish at the start and then move them around to order them into the appropriate flow for your presentation, without losing your ideas along the way.

If you colour code your stories to link with particular key points you will easily be able to see which points have many stories illustrating the message, and where you need to find more.

Using a mind map or spider diagram

The process of mind mapping was first coined by Tony Buzan and I spent a stimulating few days in Cambridge learning the technique from him one summer. My mind maps don't quite meet Tony's standard, but I do find them another excellent way of laying out a presentation.

To begin drawing your mind map, take a sheet of A4 paper and turn it landscape way round; so that the longest sides are top and bottom. Then start with your idea in the centre and draw three large spokes. These will be the main points you wish to make. From there, the three spokes each have three sub-spokes, indicating sub-points and stories to illustrate them. You can either fill out the mind map as you go, or draw the basic structure first and then complete it.

A mind map is very easy to use if you know the points and the stories you wish to use. I regularly use mind maps for presentations, even those I give often; redrawing the mind map before a presentation is a way of putting the information back into your memory for ease of recall on the day. Also, having a mind map handy when making a presentation can be a useful back-up if you wish to remind yourself of a key point; it prevents the tendency to read verbatim and still provides a memory jogger for comfort.

Too many people use their slide presentation to remind themselves of their key points; this is where 'death by PowerPoint' creeps in and is something I am strongly against. PowerPoint, as you will see in **Step 6**, is useful to provide your audience with a visual representation of your message, *not* to provide you, the presenter, with your speech. Simply knowing a mind map is available can free up your brain to focus on your audience, rather than on remembering the presentation.

There are many good software tools to help you draw your mind maps, and numerous books on the subject. But to enable me to remember my presentation, I find there is nothing better than writing out my mind map longhand, using coloured spokes; there is something about drawing and writing it out by hand, rather than typing it, that enables my brain, and maybe yours, to remember the presentation better.

The power of three

Once you have some structure to what you want to say, you are now ready to start to craft the words.

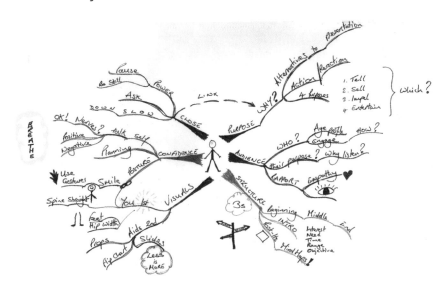

You will notice from both the Post-it and mind map examples that there are three key points, with three sub-points, each with a story. The power of three is useful to remember not only when designing your presentation, but also when crafting the words themselves.

 **Exercise**

Read the following aloud and notice the difference in rhythm and impact:

Veni, vidi, vici: I came, I saw, I conquered	vs	I came and conquered
They took the bait, hook, line and sinker	vs	They took the bait
Design, develop and deliver powerful presentations	vs	Design and deliver powerful presentations
Tried, tested and proven techniques to . . .	vs	Tested and proven techniques to . . .

The power of three, or in Latin, *omne trium perfectum* – everything that comes in threes is perfect – is also used when making key points, providing emphasis or even humour. Here are a few more examples of the power of three:

- 'There are three kinds of lies: lies, damned lies, and statistics', Mark Twain, who attributed it to Benjamin Disraeli.
- 'A government by the people, for the people, and of the people', Abraham Lincoln.
- 'Friends, Romans, countrymen, lend me your ears', Mark Antony in Shakespeare's *Julius Caesar*.
- 'There are three types of people in this world: those who make things happen, those who watch things happen and those who wonder what happened', Mary Kay Ash, American businesswoman and founder of Mary Kay Cosmetics Inc.

Watch a video showing the use of the power of three at: www.thebusinessgym.net

A more recent public figure renowned for his presentation style was Steve Jobs. Jobs became famous not only for the products he and Apple produced, but also for his style of presenting them to both the business and the wider world. In this quote and the online clip of his presentation of the iPhone you will see his use of the power of three.

> *Well, today we're introducing three revolutionary products . . . the first one is a wide screen iPod with touch controls, the second is a revolutionary mobile phone, and the third is a breakthrough internet communications device. So three things: a wide screen iPod with touch controls, a revolutionary mobile phone, and a breakthrough internet communications device. An iPod, a phone and an internet communicator. An iPod, a phone . . . are you getting it? These are not three separate devices, this is one device and we are calling it iPhone.*

Steve Jobs introducing the iPhone in 2007

This link is to a video of Steve Jobs introducing the iPhone:
www.youtube.com/watch?feature=player_embedded&v=
x7qPAY9JqE4

Exceptions to the rule

There are, of course, exceptions to any rule. How many of you, when thinking about Winston Churchill's first speech as Prime Minster to the House of Commons, remember what he had to offer the country on 14 May 1940? His words were: '*I have nothing to offer but **blood, toil, tears and sweat**.*' (Did you recall all four?)

The power of repetition

In addition to the power of three, note how repetition plays its part.

How often do you need to say something for it to be remembered? There is no definitive answer to the question as it will, of course, depend upon what it is you are saying. However, there is definite power in repetition and three times is a good place to start from.

A speech by the Burmese opposition leader Aung San Suu Kyi in 1990 used repeated words to provide powerful emphasis:

> *__Fear__lessness may be a gift, but perhaps most precious is the **courage** acquired through endeavour, **courage** that comes from cultivating the habit of refusing to let fear dictate one's actions, **courage** that could be described as '**grace** under pressure' – **grace** which is renewed repeatedly in the face of harsh, unremitting pressure.*

Churchill used repetition in most, if not all, of his speeches. Here, for instance, is a section towards the beginning of a speech to Harrow School in 1941:

> *Why when I was here last we were quite **alone**, desperately **alone**, and we had been so for five or six months. We were **poorly armed**. We are not so **poorly armed** today; but then we were very **poorly armed**.*

Winston Churchill – great orators do not need visual aids

In Martin Luther King's civil rights speech at the Lincoln Memorial on 28 August 1963 he repeated the phrase 'I have a dream' at the beginning of six sentences:

www.history.com/topics/black-history/martin-luther-king-jr/videos

Known as *anaphora* in the Greek art of rhetoric, repetition at the beginning of sentences is a powerful device for creating emphasis. Interestingly, the 'I have a dream' repetition wasn't written into King's original speech, though he had used the phrase in previous speeches; it was, amazingly, an improvised part of that speech and one that has become the most memorable.

Also consider this by Charles Dickens in *A Tale of Two Cities*:

It was the best of times, it was the worst of times, it was the age of wisdom, it was the age of foolishness, it was the epoch of belief, it was the epoch of incredulity, it was the season of Light, it was the season of Darkness, it was the spring of hope,

> ***it was** the winter of despair, **we had** everything before us, **we had** nothing before us, **we were all going direct** to Heaven, **we were all going direct** the other way . . ..*

Just in case you are wondering, the same device can be used at the end of sentences, when it is called *epiphora*.

For example:

> *She's safe, **just like I promised**. She's all set to marry Norrington, **just like she promised**. And you get to die for her, **just like you promised**.* (Jack Sparrow in the film *Pirates of the Caribbean: The Curse of the Black Pearl*)

> *There is nothing wrong **with America** that cannot be cured by what is right **with America**.* (Bill Clinton)

Signposting

As well as providing your audience with an outline at the start of your presentation, you can use particular phrases to signpost the way during your speech. This not only helps provide structure and gives your audience a sense of security, as they believe you know where you are going, it can also help you to remember your talk if you start to feel lost. Knowing a rough direction and setting out the signposts along the way assists brains to both take in the information and remember it, from both the presenter's and the listener's viewpoint.

In this section you will find some examples of signposts and when you could use them.

Useful phrases to set the scene at the beginning of your presentation:

- To begin with I'm going to outline three ways you can . . .
- To start off the discussion let's look at things from the customer's point of view . . .
- I'm going to kick off by . . .
- To start with . . . later . . . to close . . .

To move to the next point:

- Moving on . . .
- The next point I'd like to come to is . . .
- As I will demonstrate in a moment . . .

To refer back to something you or an earlier speaker said:

- As was mentioned by . . .
- As I have already mentioned . . .
- Let's go back to the point I made earlier . . .

To flag what is coming up next:

- As I'll come to shortly . . .
- In a moment we'll look at . . .
- In the last 10 minutes we'll go through . . .

To create a list, or a number of points you are going to make:

- There are three key points . . .
    o First of all . . .
    o Secondly . . .
    o Thirdly . . .

Do make sure you clearly enumerate each point as you make it; if you set it out that way at the beginning, make sure you are clear about how many points you are going to make.

I have heard presenters state that there were a certain number of points in their presentations and then only had time to talk about three when they had cited four, or had even spoken on five or six points, exceeding the number they said they were going to mention. To avoid this trap you could say that 'there are a number of points I would like to cover . . .' then use first, secondly, etc.

(Grammatically there is no such word as 'firstly', though many people use it.)

To go into more depth:

- Let's consider this in more detail . . .

To summarise your talk:

- To recap . . .
- Let's recap the main points . . .
- In summary . . .

To highlight the key point you want people to remember:

- If you remember nothing else from this presentation, remember this . . .
- The most important thing to remember is . . .

These can only be used once, which may seem obvious, but you would be surprised by how many people deliver their key message, and then follow it with another key message.

The same applies to your close:

- And finally . . .
- In summary . . .

Again beware of using these more than once. I have been guilty of drawing to an effective conclusion in a competition speech, only to think on the spur of the moment of another point I really wanted to make, and adding it in. Quite rightly this was noted by the judges to be an ineffective way of ending a talk.

There is more on how to develop your speaking skills through joining various clubs in the mentor toolkit towards the end of this book. There you will find links to organisations that offer the opportunity to practise presenting in a friendly and supportive environment, such as Toastmasters, Speakers Clubs and Junior Chamber International.

I or we - which should you use?

How many times are you using 'I' in a speech, when you could be using 'we'? Which is more appropriate?

If you are talking about something you have done, perhaps using the first person singular 'I' will be appropriate. However, if it was a team effort and your intention is to inspire the team or thank them, then using 'I' will alienate them and it will be better to use the first person plural, 'we'.

The I:we ratio is monitored by website copywriters, so why not follow Apple's founder Steve Jobs when unveiling the iPhone in 2007: '*We're* going to make some history together here today.'

Case study

For a carefully crafted speech, take a look at actress Emma Watson's speech to the United Nations on the 'HeforShe' campaign. It also shows how you can present, despite feeling nervous.

 www.youtube.com/watch?v=gkjW9PZBRfk

When viewing this speech consider the following:

- How does Emma set out the purpose of her speech?
- How quickly does she address the potential downside of the topic?
- How does Emma manage her nerves?
- Observe her use of repetition.

 **Exercise**

Create your next presentation using either a mind map or Post-its.

Add in some signposting phrases.

How has that helped you structure your presentation?

Call to action

- Structure your presentation with at least a beginning, middle and end.
- Be clear on your key messages.
- Use the power of three when crafting your words.
- Repeat key words and phrases for emphasis.
- Use verbal signposts so your audience knows where the presentation is going.
- Use 'we' rather than 'I' whenever appropriate.

Step 4
Get the opening right

After reading this step you will be able to:

- Use a framework to write your opening
- Engage your audience from the start
- Set the tone of your presentation.

In any presentation or pitch, getting the opening right is vital. As human beings we make instant judgements about people, and whether they are worth listening to, within a few seconds. In this step we will look at how to set the tone at the start of your presentation; later, in **Step 10**, we will cover the importance of how you end your presentation.

> *Tell them what you are going to tell them, tell them and then tell them what you have told them.*

This is a common structure for presentations, and when used effectively can be really useful. However, using this structure for all your presentations can be incredibly boring. Sometimes you don't want the audience to know at the start the key points of your presentation, because during the middle section you may lose people's interest if they already know exactly what you are about to cover. Likewise, while a summary is important, going through everything again can be tedious for the listener.

Don't start with an apology

After the sin of opening with 'Um . . .' some of the weakest openings start with 'I'm sorry I've not had time to prepare' or 'I'm sorry I'm not used to speaking to this size of group'.

 Never, ever, start a presentation with an apology.

Even if you haven't had time to prepare, or you are feeling nervous, or it is the first presentation you have ever given, don't apologise. Your audience are looking for you to take the lead and guide them through the next few minutes or however long your presentation will last. They want to be in safe hands, and an apology detracts from your message and makes the audience feel unsafe, making a difficult presentation even harder for you.

An apology can also convey a lack of respect for your audience if you tell them you haven't had time to prepare, however true the statement might be. I once observed an accomplished speaker give what seemed to be a great talk to a group of young professionals. Afterwards a colleague commented to me that the speaker lost her from the start when she opened up by saying that she had completed her slides in the car park just before giving the presentation. My colleague was appalled that the speaker thought so little of her audience and couldn't be bothered to prepare in advance. I hadn't taken the comment that way at all . . . but it just goes to show how careful you must be with the opening few words.

So what can you do to engage the audience at the beginning?

When I started out in training I learned a mnemonic to use at the beginning of every presentation:

INTRO

Interest – use a 'grabber' to spike the audience's interest in what you are going to say.

Need – why do the audience need to hear what you have to say?

Time – how long will your presentation last?

Range – what will you be covering?

Objectives – what will they know at the end?

Case study

A typical presentation opening might be: 'Hello, my name is. . . let me give you a little bit of background to the company and myself. . . what I want to tell you about happiness and well-being is. . . .'

Compare this with the following opening using the INTRO structure:

> *87% of the UK population would choose happiness and well-being over wealth (I). Would you like to increase your happiness and well-being? (N) In the next half an hour (T) I will cover three proven strategies (R) you can easily incorporate into your life to provide you with a happiness and well-being boost (O).*

Then, if necessary, follow with your name and a very short couple of sentences to establish your credibility on the subject before getting into the topic in detail.

Using a statistic or a question is a good technique for opening your presentation. But a word of caution, as with all techniques, it needs to be used in moderation.

If you are giving a day-long training workshop consisting of different segments every hour or so, starting the same way each time and using the INTRO structure may appear regimented. If you separate the morning and the afternoon and give an INTRO for both of those, rather than for every segment, your audience still knows what is happening, and has their interest sparked.

Alternative INTROs

Instead of a question or statistic you could use one of the following as your INTRO 'grabber':

- a cartoon or short video clip;
- a controversial statement;
- a quote from a historical figure or celebrity.

'Like religion, politics, and family planning, cereal is not a topic to be brought up in public. It's too controversial.'

A 'grabber' from the great American humourist, Erma Bombeck

Controversial statement

An example of this would be '**women have no place in the boardroom**' if you are going to discuss diversity and gender equality issues, and then to show how the attitude has changed over the years and how much further it needs to change.

Quote from historical figure

Reality is merely an illusion, albeit a persistent one. Albert Einstein

 **Exercise**

If you were to write out an INTRO for your next presentation, what would it look like?

Think of the topic of your presentation, what the audience are interested in knowing and what you want them to know or do at the end (refer back to Step 2 to remind yourself how to do this).

Interest

Needs

Time

Range

Objectives

For example, when pitching for finance most people immediately think of *Dragon's Den*.

The investor wants to know upfront how much you are asking for, so include this in your introduction. More details about presenting a concept or idea are given in **Part 2**.

Alternative openings

It is tempting to open by saying 'I have a question . . .' then proceed to state your question. However, it is much better and far more powerful to simply start with the question. As a comparison you wouldn't say, 'I'd like to make a statement . . .' and then make the statement, you would just make the statement.

In the same vein, don't begin by saying 'here's an interesting fact . . .' then state the fact. This depletes the impact and prompts the audience to think about whether the fact was interesting or not, which wasn't what you wanted them to be thinking about.

To begin a presentation powerfully, use power in both your speech and your voice. Think about the power in the opening lines of President Obama's 2008 election victory speech:

> *If there is anyone out there who still doubts that America is a place where all things are possible; who still wonders if the dream of our founders is alive in our time; who still questions the power of our democracy, tonight is your answer.*

Or President Lincoln's Gettysburg address in 1863, which opened:

> *Fourscore and seven years ago our fathers brought forth on this continent, a new nation, conceived in Liberty, and dedicated to the proposition that all men are created equal.*

Why, what, how, where and when

Another method of opening a presentation is to look at the following four elements:

1. **Why** – why you, why this topic, why for this audience, why now?

2. **What** – what will you cover, what do they already know, what will be new, what will they learn?

3. **How** – how will you address the topic, how can the audience put it into practice?

4. **Where and when** – where could this apply, when might it apply?

Let's take each of these in turn.

Why

If your audience can find a reason to listen, they are much more likely to pay attention to what you are saying. So provide them with that reason in the first sentence you utter.

For example, if you were to give a talk about the company's finances you might decide to say something like:

In the next half an hour I'm going to take you through the details of the company finances, our profit and loss and the targets for the coming year.

Some people even start their presentations with an apology for having to go through the boring financial bits. Stop. Rethink. If you tell someone what you are about to present is boring, they will switch off; who wants to listen to a boring presentation? If you can give them a reason to listen, at least they will stay engaged at the start.

So, as an alternative to the example above, how about saying:

You have all worked hard over the past 12 months and I'm sure you all want to know the impact that's had on the figures. . . .

Identifying 'why you; why this topic' is something the Canadian professional speaker, the late Warren Evans, used to cite as an important structure for an introduction. That is the introduction a master of ceremonies or chairperson might give before you start your talk. If you are without an introducer, as I suspect most of you will be, you could include this as part of your opening – after your INTRO 'grabber' of course – as a way of establishing your credibility.

What

This is the 'tell 'em what you're going to tell 'em' section; a very brief signposting on what is coming up. Often it is missed and audiences are launched straight into the content without a framework. It is a bit like setting off on a car journey with someone else driving and you are in the passenger seat blindfolded with no idea of the length, purpose or destination. Instead, to continue with the financial example, you could say something like:

There are three key figures: our turnover, our profit and our cash-flow. Rather than taking it department by department, that information will be available immediately after this presentation on the intranet. I'll walk you through the highlights.

How

This is often where the slide presentation starts, which results in internal groans, glazed eyes and switched-off brains. So instead of the usual graphics, pie charts or bar charts, can you find a different way to present your data?

Maybe not like this though

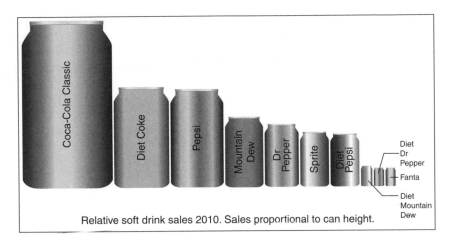

Relative soft drink sales 2010. Sales proportional to can height.

Clear and engaging
Source: https://timwit.wordpress.com/tag/drinks/

Where and when

With regard to your audience's work, where is the information you're about to present applicable? Where else does it apply?

For instance, when presenting on confidence in public speaking, I will explore with the audience when their next opportunity to practise will be. It might be an imminent presentation at work, but it could be giving honest feedback about poor service in a restaurant or praising your teenager. All of those need to be undertaken with confidence and authenticity – something we'll come onto in a moment.

 When planning your presentation, ask yourself another key question: so what?

- The company's made a profit . . . so what?
- We'll be able to invest in that new IT system . . . so what?
- You'll have increased access to customer data . . . so what?
- When a customer phones up you'll be able to provide them with a detailed answer at the press of a button . . . so what?
- Customer calls will take less time . . . so what?

- You'll have more time for doing the rest of your work . . . so what?
- Backlogs will reduce . . . so what?
- Less stress . . . so what?
- Happier workforce . . . so what?
- More productive . . . so what?
- More profit . . . so what?
- We stay in business . . . so what?
- You keep your job . . .

Get the picture? This can go on *ad infinitum*. I suggest you do it at least three times to reach a meaningful answer to the information you are about to present.

 Whichever style of opening you choose, there is another key factor to consider: *authenticity*.

You might not notice someone who is being authentic, but when inauthenticity strikes it can be smelt a mile off, like an open sewer.

If you don't feel comfortable opening up your presentation with a quote after practising it a few times, then however much you like the quote ditch it, or put it later in your presentation and decide on a different way to open.

If you are not naturally energetic don't try to be Steve Ballmer, former CEO of Microsoft, known for his highly energetic stage performances.

If you are not naturally humorous, don't try to tell jokes.

A level of authenticity is needed to help the audience connect with you as the speaker. While you do need to bring yourself out of your natural shy zone, if that is your predilection, you still need to be you.

Be congruent by making sure your message is aligned. Take the words, the way in which you say them in both emphasis and energy, as well as how you look when you say them, and make sure you are giving the same message through all

Steve Ballmer in full flow

aspects: your verbal content, the words themselves, your vocal variety, the emphasis and energy and the visual impact of your body language.

 See the digital content for examples of how to open your presentation at:

www.thebusinessgym.net

A word about Dr Albert Mehrabian

You may have been expecting to find some information about the relative importance of body language, vocal tone and words in this book. Dr Albert Mehrabian of UCLA, author of *Silent Messages: Implicit Communication of Emotions and Attitude*, completed a number of studies in this area which have sadly been misconstrued, generalised and popularised in communications training. While words convey important messages, so does our body language and our tone of voice. However, Mehrabian's research only looked at the communication of feelings and attitudes, not information or knowledge. So even though an advertising agency once claimed that a certain credit card said more about you than you ever could because 93% of communication was non-verbal, this isn't backed up by science.

 Learn more about Albert Mehrabian and his work here:
http://en.wikipedia.org/wiki/Albert_Mehrabian

www.kaaj.com/psych/index.html

 **Exercise**

Time for reflection

Go to the website **www.ted.com** (Ideas Worth Spreading) and pick three talks at random. Listen to the first few minutes of the talks and answer the following questions:

- What caught your attention?
- What lost your interest?
- Why?
- What do your observations tell you about your next presentation?

Call to action

Do

- Use INTRO – Interest, Need, Time, Range, Objectives – to plan your beginning:
  - o or a cartoon, video clip, controversial statement or quote;
  - o or use Why, What, How, Where and When.
- Look up before you speak.
  - o Learn the first couple of sentences by heart.
  - o Rehearse your opening, even if you have no time to rehearse anything else.

Don't

- Start with 'Um. . .'
- Start with 'So. . .'
- Start with an apology.

Step 5

Get your audience involved

After reading this step you will be able to:

- Create a two-way discussion
- Interact with your audience
- Make it memorable.

One of the questions I'm often asked is how much content to put into a talk. It depends on your audience, the purpose of your speech and any specific requests from the person who asked you to give the talk. With those caveats, in this step you will find guidelines on balancing your content, including stories and getting your audience involved.

To quote the novelist George Orwell:

> *A scrupulous writer, in every sentence that he writes, will ask themselves at least four questions, thus:*
>
> - *What am I trying to say?*
> - *What words will express it?*
> - *What image or idiom will make it clearer?*
> - *Is this image fresh enough to have an effect?*
>
> *And he will probably ask himself two more:*
>
> - *Could I put it more shortly?*
> - *Have I said anything that is avoidably ugly?*
>
> *In addition:*
>
> - *Never use a long word where a short one will do.*
> - *If it is possible to cut a word out, always cut it out.*
> - *Never use the passive where you can use the active.*
> - *Never use a foreign phrase, a scientific word, or a jargon word if you can think of an everyday English equivalent.*
>
> *Break any of these rules sooner than say anything outright barbarous!*
>
> *Source*: From *Politics and the English Language* by George Orwell

Make it memorable

Storytelling is a very powerful way of getting a message across. Stories appeal to our emotions and therefore create memorable images in our brains. They can also remind us of feeling safe and receptive to information and so could be a way to get across what might otherwise be directive messages by leaving the audience to figure out the moral of the story.

Good stories have a point. Bad stories meander, are full of waffle and often serve the storyteller's ego rather than benefit the listener.

To make a point stories need just enough detail, but not too much, and often make a connection with the emotions of the listener.

One story I use when talking about a manager making time to engage with their staff is about the time I experienced a less than 30-second encounter with my boss. It goes like this:

> *My granddad had been killed in a car accident (pause). The next day I was at work and the director I was working for at the time passed me in the corridor (pause). He stopped (pause), touched my elbow (pause) and said 'I'm sorry to hear your news' (pause). It can take just a few seconds to create a lasting connection, it doesn't have to be a long conversation . . .*

And I might add on the question: when did you last make a connection with your staff?

I could tell that story in more detail, including the date, day of the week, name of the company I was working for, the director's name and the job I was doing at the time, the fact we were actually walking through the downstairs office of the bank, and how welled up I felt. *But* the detail would get in the way of the point.

So if you are tempted to tell a story, and I would encourage you to do so, know the point you want to make. Ensure your story is long enough to make the point and succinct enough not to cloud it.

The other thing to notice about this story is that it is personal. It really happened to me. I am not telling someone else's story as if it happened to me, nor am I telling a generic story to make a point.

There are many generic stories that can be used to make a point, but none of them can beat a personal story for impact. I have found a book called *Tales for Trainers* by Margaret Parkin a useful reference. There are many examples of how to use stories and metaphors to facilitate learning included in that book and there are times when they come in handy. But use them sparingly, as the most powerful stories come from your own experience.

I suggest you start to build a list of stories in a notebook, or on a file stored on your laptop or other device, which you can use. That way, you won't find someone switching off from your presentation because they've heard the generic story before.

When telling stories be in the moment, don't just retell the story. Put it into your own words and make it come alive. Make sure you choose your stories according to the length of your presentation. Don't use a long story for a short presentation. If you have a couple of hours then a few long stories peppered with shorter ones might work well.

 Develop a bank of your own personal stories and metaphors to make your presentation unique.

Here are a few examples of metaphors:

A reader's comment on the website of the Yale statistician, Edward Tufte, contains a powerful metaphor to express his view on sharing PowerPoint slides: *'I would no more share a presentation than I would a toothbrush.'* What emotion does that evoke? Possibly disgust at the thought of sharing a toothbrush. So will you now share other people's presentations in the future? Possibly not, or only with good reason and with caution.

The comment also reminded me of another analogy from my early days as a training manager. I remember being advised by my mentor that not leaving a training room tidy, including taking used paper off the flip chart, was like going to the toilet and not flushing it. So that is why I now always strip used paper from a flipchart!

Toothbrushes and toilets are *universal experiences* that everyone can relate to. However, taking the experience of white-water rafting, for instance, to illustrate fear or excitement, will only work with those who have been white-water rafting, so we need to be careful with the scope of our analogies.

Alternatively you can use a visually evocative metaphor. These examples are from the novel *The Snow Geese* by William Fiennes, who uses many metaphors in his writing:

> Snug in their cubbyholes like whelks in their conches.

> Sounds rolled round the bowl of the hills like balls in a roulette wheel.

A tip for saving and categorising your stories

Use a note-taking system, such as Evernote, which is available online for free, and add tags to your stories to make them searchable by category. If you are of a more traditional bent then index cards or a notebook will serve the purpose.

Discussion: involving the audience

Having some form of audience participation helps to keep the audience interested in your presentation. From rhetorical questions, to show of hands, to full-on discussions there are various ways you can involve your audience.

Rhetorical questions

The power of rhetorical questions is that you are encouraging your audience to think about your topic without spending lots of time getting feedback from them. It kicks their brains into mulling over the topic in a new way rather than just being in receiver mode.

If you ask a rhetorical question make sure you leave a pause to allow the audience to think through their answer, but gauging it short enough to ensure no one answers it aloud can be tricky.

If someone does answer it aloud, it is important to react and reply appropriately to their response. Make your audience feel welcome and safe, not threatened. Replying by saying there was no need for them to respond, or that you were just asking the question rhetorically, is really putting down your audience member. Thank them for responding, in the same way you would if you had meant a response to be forthcoming.

Of course you can phrase a rhetorical question to indicate no response is necessary, by using the following phrases, or others you can think of:

- Just think for a moment, when did you last . . .
- There's no need to answer this aloud, but who here has . . .
- Take a moment to reflect; how will you use this . . .

Issues to watch out for

If you allow your audience to go into a discussion, while it is a great way to get them involved it is also a possible way to lose them. Discussions can become heated, or drift off topic.

A break for discussion isn't a break for you as the presenter. You need to keep a close eye on how the discussion is going. Listen in to what is being said by moving through your audience. If you notice the discussion going off track you may need to bring them back, either as whole group or by speaking to the individuals concerned.

Having a method for bringing the audience back that has been agreed in advance is also useful. I like to use a Tibetan singing bowl, which I think makes a kinder sound than a whistle or drum sticks, both of which I've seen used by others. But occasionally I find someone in the audience who doesn't like the sound, so I need to think of another way. One alternative is for the facilitator to say 'shh' to one person who passes it to the people around

You've lost control if your audience does this

them. Once someone receives the 'shh' they stay quiet and the 'shh' spreads through the room like ripples in a pond. You can also have fun by challenging the group to see how quickly they can spread it through the whole room. I first saw this used by John Cremer, an expert in improvisation techniques. This method saves you shouting 'shh' over everyone's voices and potentially becoming hoarse.

Injecting humour

Only do this if you are naturally humorous. If, like me, you didn't get the 'humorous gene' at birth, it may not be a good idea to try to copy those who did. The humour in my speeches comes when I stumble upon it, often ad lib or when responding to an audience reaction.

However, for those of you willing to take the risk, humour can be purposefully injected into a speech. The rule of three can help you do this.

When using humour, the first two statements set a pattern and the third breaks the pattern, thereby prompting a laugh from your audience as they see the unexpected.

 See the online content for more information on using humour and stories:

www.thebusinessgym.net

Case study

For an example of humour, the educationalist Sir Ken Robinson has presented a couple of excellent talks at TED Conferences (regular international meetings focused on 'ideas worth spreading'). In one he opens with a humorous compliment to the previous speakers: *'Good morning, it's been great hasn't it. . .? I've been blown away by the whole thing. . . in fact I'm leaving. . . .'* It is all in the timing, the look on his face and the unexpected statement.

Watch his talk here: **www.ted.com/talks/ken_robinson_says_ schools_kill_creativity**.

 **Exercise**

What universal experiences can you use in your presentations? Add your own to the list below.

It's like when. . .

- you take that first lick of the ice cream cone;
- the sun warms your back;
- you walk barefoot on the beach;
- you find a spider in the bath;
- you've been bitten by a mosquito;
- you're in a crowded lift (elevator).

Call to action

- Find your own personal stories.
- Connect through emotions.
- Use metaphors.
- Inject humour with care.
- Keep control of discussions.

Step 6

Use of visual aids, body language and dress codes

After reading this step you will be able to:
- Convey your message through body language
- Create effective visual aids and alternatives to slides
- Use technology wisely.

When thinking about using visual aids, the first thing that comes to mind tends to be the ubiquitous use of slides. This step will cover some of the dos and don'ts of PowerPoint, but there is so much more to visual aids. Depending on what it is you are presenting, you may have a prop, such as a prototype model or other illustrative piece of equipment, to enhance your talk. Or you may wish to write key points that crop up onto a flipchart. But by far the biggest visual aid to a presentation is you; your body language speaks volumes. So it is really important to ensure that your body is congruent with your message. During this step I will endeavour to provide pointers in all of these areas, and there is much more online where you can see video clips of what to do and what to avoid.

Let's start with dress codes and body language

When planning your presentation, remember that *you* are a visual aid. Your audience will be looking at you, which is what some people find so off-putting in presentations. If that is the case for you, make sure you read **Step 9** on confidence.

Human beings are naturally judgemental, and while I don't know anyone who actively wants to see someone fail while making a presentation, I do know people will critique the presenter's appearance, not just their content.

So what do you wear when giving a presentation? There are no hard and fast rules; it depends on the purpose of your presentation, the importance of it, the environment and culture and how you feel. If you are giving a regular team briefing there is no need to dress any differently from your norm. However, if you are presenting on a stage to a large audience you might want to dress 'up'. By that I mean wear your best suit or a dress, possibly a tie, polish your shoes, tidy your hair, shave your stubble, put on a jacket. However, you can ignore all of those suggestions if the culture or business etiquette says differently.

For instance, at a conference I attended, the keynote speaker turned up wearing jeans, a denim shirt and had an earring and a ponytail. Guess the profession? IT. He was totally congruent with his brand, and during his talk referenced the fact that he, as MD, wore the same as all of his employees. However, I have seen another keynote speaker turn up to a dinner engagement who was the only one not wearing black tie (tuxedo). He hadn't been advised of the dress code and seemed quite uncomfortable because he mentioned it as he started his talk (in that situation I would suggest he didn't mention his dress at all).

Check out the dress code in advance. If it is a work-based presentation then wear something you feel good in, not just comfortable. Ensure you are congruent with your message and the image you want to portray. Also, if you are going to wear a microphone, make sure there's somewhere to hang the battery pack (see the section on technology later in this step).

Body language and gestures

Use of body language in a presentation is one of the most effective visual aids. Take a look at where you can use gestures, how much room you will have to manoeuvre and where you can 'place' certain messages as you physically move to those areas.

Simple examples are gesturing from left to right for past and future tense. But be careful to switch to take into account the audience's view. When making a gesture to indicate how far the organisation, team or product has come that would be in the past. Typically in the West we indicate the past on our left. However, if you did that when speaking in front of an audience it would be to their right, i.e. in their future. So as a speaker remember to swap them around. Speak about how far something has come by a gesture to your right. Then indicate how far you want to go by making a gesture into the future; in this case as a speaker it will be to your left.

When you first do this it will feel counter-intuitive, but it is surprisingly effective from the audience's point of view, even if they don't consciously realise it.

Other obvious gestures are to indicate size, height, up or down. When making a presentation, keep in mind the size of your audience and the size of the room you are in. This will affect the size of your gestures. If you are in a small meeting room with two other people, making a very large, outstretched gesture to indicate maximum capacity with both arms would be overdoing it a bit. Yet if you are on a stage speaking to, say, 50 or more people then a large outstretched gesture is perfectly appropriate. Indeed, a small gesture wouldn't create the desired impact.

When you are not making a gesture with your hands they can be kept by your side, or loosely interlinked by your waist with your elbows bent.

Do not put your hands in your pockets and do not clasp them in a fig-leaf position in front of your groin or behind your back in a sergeant-major style.

While mentioning pockets, it is always a good idea to clear your pockets of any coins and keys before a presentation as they make a distracting chinking sound when fiddled with. This will ensure that if you are a fiddler you won't find anything to fiddle with.

Be wary of pointing

I am often asked whether gestures are appropriate to make. Many people have been told that when giving a presentation they should stand still and keep their arms by their sides. I may be biased, as my own natural style is to gesticulate, but I can't think of a more unnatural way to make a presentation than to remain static. Though be wary of pointing with your index finger as it often takes people back to being told off, either at school or by their parents, and isn't necessarily a reaction you wish to evoke.

If you are speaking from behind a lectern, and that is where the only microphone is situated, bear in mind that the audience cannot see gestures at waist height. You will need to make them above the height of the lectern, or decide not to make them at all.

Lecterns provide a danger all of their own. Depending on your personal height, they can afford a cosy place to stand, engulf you if you are short or, if you are tall, the microphone might only just pick up the sound of your voice. This is something to consider when planning your presentation under the 'where' section. Coming out from behind a lectern can be useful, but not if you have no lapel mic and a quiet voice, or if there is a lot of background noise, as no one will be able to hear you. In some lecture theatres the projector hangs from the ceiling, and while you may not be aware of the noise it could impact on the ability of the audience to hear you clearly. Also, even if you are able to project your voice loudly, keep in mind that someone in your audience might have hearing difficulties or the length of your presentation may mean that constant projection for a long time is wearing on your voice.

Following on from physical hand gestures, it is definitely worth keeping in mind facial expressions. Keep them appropriate to the content of your talk. You wouldn't commiserate with a friend on the death of their pet by smiling, would you?

Smiles, frowns, grimaces, nervous ticks, flicks of the hair, scratching of noses or chins, widening of or screwing up eyes all impact your message – they can enhance or detract from it.

Standing still is unnatural, so do move during your presentation, but try not to pace or prowl.

Dos and don'ts

- Do move with purpose.
- Don't lean on one leg.
- Do move your weight to move your feet.
- Don't cross your legs or ankles when standing – it's surprising how many people do.
- Do keep your feet equally weighted about hip-width apart when you want to make a key point.
- Don't pace or prowl (i.e. like a caged lion).

In the West, slow gestures indicate gravitas and knowledge whereas fast gestures instil excitement and enthusiasm. Some interesting research in this area has been carried out by non-verbal communications expert Michael Grinder. See **Step 9** on confidence, which draws on some of Michael's findings.

A final word on posture relates to the spine. Keeping yourself upright is so important and I see too many people who slouch, hunch or shrug when making presentations. This tends to give the impression you are feeling uncomfortable. Standing tall indicates that you are in charge, that you know what you want to say and that you have a message to put across that should be listened to.

 There is more to body language than meets the eye. Your posture not only impacts on your message, but it also affects your emotions. Social psychologist Amy Cuddy has given a talk on the findings of her research, which identified some power poses that boost self-confidence, and also explanations of poses not to use: www.ted.com/talks/amy_cuddy_your_ body_language_shapes_who_you_are?language=en

See the online content for ideas of what to do with your hands, how to stand and appropriate use of gestures: www.thebusinessgym.net

PowerPoint tips

While this book doesn't focus on PowerPoint, nevertheless it needs a mention as many people think a presentation is synonymous with creating a PowerPoint presentation. As has already been mentioned, that is not the case. However, here are a few tips for using PowerPoint effectively, and for more on the topic see the Bibliography and further reading section for other book recommendations.

Slide design

To design your slides it is not a good idea to choose from Microsoft's default presentation options. They tend to look rather dull and uninspiring and will be very similar to everyone else's presentations, so you won't stand out. However, you may have a company default you have to adhere to; sadly this is often based on what I have just said not to do. You'll need to follow your company branding and stick to the corporate colours, but if you do have a free hand then I recommend using a dark background and white text. This gives a dark screen, which is much less tiring on the eyes for an audience and keeps the audience's focus on you, rather than on a bright screen behind you. Any press or PR photographers in the audience will also thank you for not having their images washed out by a bright, shiny screen.

If white on dark is good enough for Apple. . .

Use of bullet points

Beware of using bullet points; the slides are an *aide-mémoire* for your audience to enhance your message, not for you as the speaker to read from. One of the worst, but most common, presentation sins is to put too much text onto a slide and then turn your back to the audience to read what is there. Your audience can read for themselves; they need you as a presenter to embellish what the slide says, not to reiterate it.

One excuse I often come across for putting lots of detail onto the slides is that they form a hand-out and are for the audience to take away and read later. There is *never* a good reason for cramming slides full of data or packed with bullet points. If you do want to make a presentation for your audience to take away later then the answer is to produce two versions of the presentation: one for the slide show and another detailed set as a hand-out.

For webinars or other online slide shows where your audience isn't present, my suggestion is to use more slide content, but spread across more slides. That way you will be changing slides more frequently, which helps to keep your audience engaged, along with good vocal variety and interaction through rhetorical questions, as mentioned in **Step 5**.

For presentations where you are in front of your audience in person, you can have the same slide up for a much longer time than if you are presenting remotely.

How many slides should I have?

There is no definitive answer to the question 'how many slides should I have for a 10-minute presentation?', or 'how many bullet points on a slide?', or 'how many words per bullet point?', It is a mix of personal preference and what suits your material.

Some have suggested that a guideline of seven bullet points, plus or minus two, is a good place to start, but that is based on erroneous extrapolation from research on memorising nonsense.

 I'll let Edward Tufte explain in this link:

www.edwardtufte.com/bboard/q-and-a-fetch-msg? msg_id=0000U6.

If you are unsure how many slides to include, err on the side of caution and reduce the number of slides, don't add slides to compensate for your worry about not having enough to say. It is much better to finish early rather than to have to rush through slides to finish on time, or even worse overrun and eat into another presenter's time or the audience's coffee break.

My personal preference is to use pictures on slides – either ones I have taken myself, royalty free images or those purchased with permission to use commercially. Good quality pictures can be enlarged to the full size of the screen, bled to the edges, which means no background showing. However, if you use a black background and don't make your pictures the full size of the screen, it isn't noticeable as the black background simply blends with the darkness of the rest of the screen.

To include a comment on your pictures, insert a text box to add a word or two if necessary.

Never put pictures, or graphs for that matter, onto your slides that, when projected, are too small for your audience to see.

I inwardly groan when someone says, 'I know this slide is a bit busy but. . . .' Or worse, 'I know you won't be able to read this, but. . . .'

 If it is too busy, *cut some out.*

 If it is too small to read, *enlarge it.*

And don't wave the laser pointer at the screen when speaking in a large venue in the hope that the poor souls at the back will spot the little red dot dancing round the screen. If you know you will need to highlight something in the text, use PowerPoint's transition feature to add an arrow, enlarge that section onto the subsequent slide, or put a box around the item you want the audience to pay attention to.

Often you will be constrained in your PowerPoint design and have to use a corporate font, but given the choice I like to use

Arial Black. This is a bold font and stands out well against different backgrounds. The font size I use most of the time is a minimum of 44, or sometimes larger depending on the slide. Small fonts will strain the eyes of your audience and they may give up listening to your presentation altogether.

To animate or not to animate?

Beware that fancy animations can be very distracting to watch, especially for an audience not brought up on fast-paced video games. The maxim of KISS is well worth keeping in mind here: Keep It Simple (Stupid). Don't use your presentation as a vehicle to show what an advanced PowerPoint pilot you are.

The number of options on transitions and animations is mind-blowing. If you have your data flying in from the left and the right, twirling in the middle, before settling still only to fade away on a chequerboard effect as you move on to the next slide, then your audience will watch the show rather than concentrate on the message you are trying to communicate.

You should be particularly sensitive to this issue if you use the Prezi Cloud Computing presentation system. Prezi offers the ability to fly through your information in 3D and allows stunning presentations to be created, in the right hands. But in the wrong hands you might need to have a supply of sick bags due to the motion sickness it can cause.

 Here is just one of many examples of using Prezi available on the internet: www.kingsfund.org.uk/topics/nhs-reform/ health-and-social-care-act-2012-timeline

For more examples of good and bad slide presentations, see the online content: www.thebusinessgym.net

If you are using slides, a remote clicker will give you the flexibility to move around, emphasise points and make a connection with your audience, rather than having to rely on the enter button or the arrow keys on the keyboard to move your slides onwards. At the risk of stating the obvious, get to know your clicker before you start. Check it works, and know which button is back and which is forward. Some even have a handy blank button on the clicker that turns the screen black, or a freeze option that allows you to view the slides coming up in your presentation while your audience still see the current slide. If you have a table or lectern, put down the clicker when you are not using it. This will prevent the tendency to wave it in the air when making a gesture, which can come across like a school teacher pointing to the class.

Face your audience

The other big danger with using slides is the natural tendency to turn away from your audience. To avoid this, either have your laptop positioned where you can see it so you know which slide is showing, or glance back and then keep your attention focused on the audience. You should know your presentation well enough to be able to click through some slides without needing to even look at what is showing on the screen (although that assumes the technology is still working, but your audience's faces will tell you if anything is amiss).

Flipcharts

Facing your audience also applies when using flipcharts. There is a great tendency to keep talking while you are writing, but that means your back is turned and people are unlikely to hear what you are saying.

While on the subject of flipcharts, they can make a welcome break from slides and allow your audience to feel you are more responsive to their needs. If you like using flipcharts, I suggest you invest in your own pens and carry them around with you. A set of magnum markers, extra-large pens, is also worth buying especially for using flipcharts with large groups.

Be aware of the colour you write in and ensure it stands out and is legible. Don't write in red pen, as it is very hard to read, but do use red for highlighting. Write by moving your elbow rather than your wrist for a better script, and write much larger than you normally would.

Technology issues

If you are using slides, don't rely on the technology working. Most of the time it does, but there could be an occasion where things don't work out.

One of the nightmares of presenters is arriving in the room and finding an IT problem with the projector. These can often be blindingly obvious issues; more than once I've arrived at a venue to find no projector at all, because 'someone has borrowed it'. Thankfully this is much less common now that projectors have fallen in price and are often built in to meeting rooms rather than sitting on a table. At the other extreme are the subtle problems where everything is connected correctly and yet the projector just won't display your laptop's screen, despite the best efforts of everyone in the room and the IT department. Again this problem is much rarer now than in the early days of electronic slide projection, as both projectors and PC software have improved their 'plug and play' capabilities enormously.

Nevertheless, the value of having plenty of time to set up, and having a fall-back if the IT fails, can be vital to handling problems calmly and allowing you to start your presentation in a collected manner, rather than being stressed and flustered by the anxiety of firefighting technical problems.

At the moment there are three basic options for conveying your precious electronic slides to the meeting:

- memory stick or external hard drive;
- taking your own laptop;
- using cloud storage, such as Dropbox, GoogleDrive or iCloud.

Check with the organiser beforehand which is their preferred method, but then use all three to give yourself back-ups.

Points to watch out for include the following.

Memory stick

- File compatibility issues: particularly if the PC in the meeting room has older software and your file was created using a newer version, say, of PowerPoint. So use 'save as' to save in an older format as well, as an insurance policy.
- Apple Mac and Windows PC compatibility issues: this is still a significant issue if you use a Mac to create PowerPoint presentations. For instance, you may find that the font is different on a PC, images are missing or embedded videos won't play. To avoid these problems you need to follow a set of compatibility guidelines. These can be found on the internet, for instance at: **www.ehow.com/how_5801689_convert-mac-powerpoint-pc-powerpoint.html**

There are also issues going the other way, which could happen if you create your presentation on a PC but are presenting in an organisation that is exclusively Apple based. This is most likely in the creative industries, but it is probably worth asking the question beforehand just to be safe.

Laptop

- There are two areas to watch when you take your own laptop, the first being physical connectors. It is still the case that nearly all projectors will be cabled up with the long-standing VGA connector. You should make sure you have this connector, or an adaptor to it, with you, particularly if you have a tablet device or a newer laptop that only has HDMI or DVI connectors.

- The other issue is persuading your device to put out the screen display on the connector as well as the screen and to get the projector to notice it. The latter might be a pain on very old projectors, but generally they automatically detect the signal and display it. Unfortunately, different laptop manufacturers use different function keys for this feature; it could be Fn + F3, F4, F5, F7, F8 or F9, so make sure you know which one works for your laptop. In Windows 7 and 8, pressing the Windows and P keys together brings up this handy menu; 'Duplicate' is the option you want:

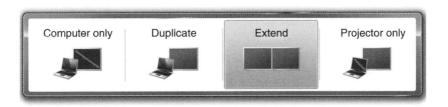

Cloud storage

- If you use cloud storage as your only means of accessing your presentation then you are relying on having an internet connection in the meeting room. For this reason, cloud storage is probably best used as a back-up option, unless you are absolutely sure that an internet connection will be available – for instance, for internal presentations where you already have all of the log-on credentials for the network.

Projector control

If you have a remote control for the projector, you can use it to access features that can add professionalism to your presentation. For example:

- When you want the audience to be paying attention to you, not the screen, you can use the 'blank' key on the remote to turn off the display for a while. (Don't turn the projector off to do this as you will have an embarrassing wait while it warms up when you want it again.) Or press B on the keyboard, which blanks the screen. You can also achieve this effect by inserting blank slides into your slide deck, although that needs more pre-planning.

- It is not good practice, but if you need to fiddle with the laptop to open up a different file, use the 'freeze' key if your remote control has one. This locks the screen so that your audience doesn't see that sensitive email that you happen to have been reading just before the presentation. Just don't forget to press 'freeze' again to unlock the screen, otherwise you are going to have a very confused audience as you gaily talk about slides only you can see on your laptop. In PowerPoint 2010 there is also a 'presenter view' in the slide show menu, which allows you to see your notes as well as edit slides during a presentation.

- If only part of the laptop screen is being displayed by the projector, the easiest solution is to adjust the screen resolution of the laptop. On a Windows PC, right click on the desktop to find the screen resolution menu.

- If the projector is sitting on a table top, don't be afraid to use the menu button to access the keystone controls that allow you to make the display rectangular even when the projector is pointing at an angle. The human brain is easily distracted by a distorted or out-of-focus display, which you can do without.

Short cuts

Here are some of the handy keyboard short cuts if using a PC:

- F5 starts the presentation from the beginning.
- Shift + F5 starts the presentation from the current slide.
- Press B to show/hide black screen.
- Press W to show/hide white screen.
- To skip over slides, type the number of the slide you want to move to and press Enter.
- Esc exits the slide show.

- Have a blank slide at the very end of your presentation. That way when you have finished, if your audience asks you questions you won't have the issue of your laptop screen showing on the main screen, it will simply be a blank slide until you are ready to exit the presentation.

Have a back-up plan

I was speaking at a dentistry conference and sent my slides through in advance, as requested by the organisers. I checked to confirm they had been received and that all was well. When I arrived at the venue the person assigned to meet me hadn't received my slides from the organiser. Luckily, or perhaps because I am a 'belt and braces' type of person, I had put my slides both onto a USB stick and into Dropbox, so we were able to access them in time for my presentation.

Microphones

I have often seen people spurn the use of microphones on the basis that they have a loud voice and can project. That may be so, but there might also be some in the audience who are hard of hearing and the PA system could make all the difference to them. Also, why would you want to shout and strain your voice? Please don't spurn the use of microphones, but there are certain things to watch out for.

The biggest issue is feedback from walking too close to the speakers. Test the mic in advance and know the range within which you are able to wander and when feedback might kick in.

'Popping' is another issue; plosive consonants such as P or B can cause a microphone to generate a popping sound, which interferes with your message. A foam windshield is needed to cure this problem, but if your lapel mic doesn't have a windshield a good tip is to clip the mic on upside down. This works really well to dampen the plosives and reduce popping.

If you know you are likely to use a mic, wear something that the battery back can either be attached to or a jacket with a pocket that it can be placed in. I have seen women with the battery pack clipped behind their neck, which is not an elegant look. Also, be prepared for the cable to be fed up the inside of a shirt, dress, jacket or even sleeve to allow it to be clipped in a suitable place.

Another point, particularly for women, is to watch for any necklaces or scarves that may catch on the microphone. I have inadvertently had a pendant catch on the microphone, which caused some distraction for the audience until I realised what the problem was. Men should watch out for their ties, which can also be an issue.

Use of props

If you are going to use props, make sure they are large enough to be seen by your audience. Don't hide them in a supermarket bag as that involves a need to rustle around while you extract the prop and causes a distraction for your audience. Either have the prop in full view, or use an upturned box, or perhaps a cloth, if you need to keep it hidden and your prop doesn't fit into a pocket.

When showing your prop to the audience, be sure to hold it up and hold it still. Waving it around is not only distracting, it also prevents people from seeing clearly what you are showing.

For large audiences, consider whether it would be worthwhile to have your prop enlarged. For instance, if you are using a prototype could your engineering department mock up an enlarged version for show? Or do you need to do what the founder of Raspberry Pi did at a conference I attended and pass round the audience an actual Raspberry Pi? This was just after they had been launched and he clearly stated he needed it returned at the end of his talk.

The danger of passing a prop round your audience isn't just losing the prop; it is also in losing the audience's attention. As the Raspberry Pi neared my seat I most definitely wasn't listening to the speaker! In addition, you never know how long the object is going to be out there doing the rounds and distracting people.

Case study

Breaking the rules

Rules for using slides and keeping your audience engaged are there to be broken, in certain circumstances and by certain people. I remember seeing one speaker who broke nearly every presentation rule there is, yet still held the audience's rapt attention. He was Edward de Bono, an expert on lateral thinking, who spoke at a conference in 2005. He came on stage, sat down, used an overhead projector instead of slides and hand wrote the acetates.

So how did he keep the audience's attention? He used a lot of interaction through discussion, questions and comments and spoke with great passion about his subject. That is what made it engaging.

 **Exercise**

Review your slide presentation

- Where can you add pictures?
- What happens if you remove all the bullet points and have two or three key words per slide with a photograph illustrating your point?

Call to action

You are the best visual aid. Ensure your body language matches your presentation:

- Smile.
- Use gestures.
- Face your audience.
- Consider using flipcharts as well as slides.
- Don't pace, shuffle or sway.
- Don't lean on the lectern or hide behind it.

Visual aids:

- Choose pictures over bullet points.
- Less is more; if in doubt, cut it out.
- Create a checklist of things to take, and things to take away again.
- Know how to set up your laptop to work with a projector.
- Plan for any Mac/PC compatibility issues beforehand.
- Don't over use animation or fancy transitions.

Step 7

Improve the clarity of your presentation

After reading this step you will be able to:

- Reduce wordiness to increase clarity
- Pause for power
- Present a persuasive argument.

Many speeches or presentations try to cram in the speaker's whole knowledge on the subject. It is impossible to tell someone everything you know on a particular subject, so don't even try.

This step covers the power of simplicity, including tips on using fewer words, the benefit of using simple language and the effect of no words at all . . . yes, silence.

Less is more

The maxim of 'less is more' applies to negotiations and presentations . . . as well as chocolate dessert.

When preparing your presentation, consider the following questions:

- What are the key points you need to make?
- How will you make them?
- What can you leave out?

Once you have written your presentation, take the metaphorical knife into the editing suite and leave everything that is superfluous on the cutting room floor. Churchill is said to have remarked:

I'm going to make a long speech because I've not had the time to prepare a short one.

The Spartans of ancient Greece were known for their terse ripostes. For example, after invading most of Greece and threatening Sparta, the Macedonians sent a message to Sparta: 'If we invade Laconia (a region of Sparta) you will be destroyed, never to rise again.' The Spartan leaders replied with a single word: 'If.' Hence the 'less is more' approach came to be called laconic.

But be careful with your laconic phrasing. I can recall listening to a short presentation in which a manager was announcing corporate changes that would allow staff to take more responsibility. The speaker used the phrase 'less handholding' without further explanation. This resulted in a barrage of difficult questions at the end of his presentation as the staff thought he meant that they would be left unsupported and abandoned – the opposite of the speaker's intention.

There needs to be enough explanation to make matters clear to your listeners, but without too much to confuse them.

This comes into play particularly when you are aiming to persuade your audience. Providing too many reasons can be counter-productive, but having one main argument, and giving various examples of how that one reason will work in practice, can be highly persuasive.

Avoid filler words

Either through nerves, or through a mannerism, some people use lots of filler words. I used to use 'actually' a lot, actually. It actually had the effect of detracting from my message rather than placing the emphasis where I actually wanted it to be. Having worked hard to reduce its use over many years, 'actually' rarely makes an appearance these days.

Listen out for your own filler words. Common ones are:

- like
- so
- basically
- obviously.

And of course:

- um
- err.

This is where listening to an audio recording of a presentation can be really helpful, as we tend not to hear our own filler words when we are speaking.

What to do if you spot filler words

If you find you are using filler words, there are a couple of steps you can take to reduce their use:

1. Become aware of the word and, each time you start to say it, stop and change what you are saying.

2. Use pauses more often. Filler words provide the equivalent of a pause by giving thinking time; use a pause instead and allow your audience to have the thinking time as well.

Recording your own talks and having them transcribed is a very good way of identifying the tendency to use filler words, or being observed by someone primed to notice your use of filler words. While recording may seem an extreme length to go to, the use of smartphones allows a recording to be made easily, and you can listen back at leisure. It may be excruciating to hear your own voice, or to watch yourself on video, but it is an extremely good way to learn how you come across and also to see what the audience sees.

Reducing wordiness

It can be tempting to write out a presentation and then read the script, especially if you are feeling nervous. But if you have ever listened to someone who has taken that approach, you will know that the written word and the spoken word don't use the same grammar, sentence structure or even vocabulary.

How many words a minute should you speak?

When writing out your speech, it is useful to have an idea of how fast you speak, but also to bear in mind that the audience need time to take in your information. If you were a documentary maker, or film maker, you would probably use the three-word-per-second guide. That translates into 180 words a minute (wpm). You'll find on the internet various statistics quoted, from 100 wpm up to 190 wpm. I have found when making a presentation that an average of 150 wpm works well, but it may be different for you. Remember, this also includes pauses, breathing and dramatic emphasis on words.

Speaking too quickly can be interpreted as nervousness by the listener. If you speed up at a certain point in your talk it can also be misconstrued as deception; an assumption may be made that you, as the speaker, were lying at that particular point. Speaking too slowly can indicate, or induce, boredom.

Exercise

Here is an exercise to enable you to practise your rate of speech. Set a timer on your watch, phone or other device to bleep when a minute is up. Then read the following aloud while timing it:

The brain and thoughts

Every time you have a thought, the biochemical/ electromagnetic resistance along the pathway carrying that thought is reduced. It is like trying to clear a path through a forest. The first time is a struggle because you have to fight your way through the undergrowth. The second time you travel that way will be easier because of the clearing you did on your first journey. The more times you travel that path, the less resistance there will be, until, after many repetitions, you have a wide, smooth track which requires little or no clearing. A similar function occurs in your brain: the more you repeat patterns or maps of thought, the less resistance there is to them. Therefore, and of greater significance, repetition itself increases the probability of repetition. In other words the more times a 'mental event' happens the more likely it is to happen again.

Source: From Buzan, T. (1995) *The Mind Map Book: Radiant Thinking – Major Evolution in Human Thought.* London: BBC Books, page 29.

How did you do? Did you finish speaking before your timer went? If so, you could slow down a little. There are some long words at the start of the passage, how easy did you find it to say them? It is important to read your own presentation aloud, even if it is not written out in detail; present it to someone, even your dog. This will help you get a feel for the words, identify where pauses are needed to aid understanding and which words to emphasise. If you find you stumble over the pronunciation of certain words, find an alternative (use a thesaurus if necessary).

 You'll find an example of this exercise demonstrated in the online content:

www.thebusinessgym.net

The power of the pause

Following on from the rate-of-speech exercise, it is not simply how fast you speak. You could speak at a very measured pace, but come across as boring simply because there is no variety or emphasis in your vocals.

 Taking pauses, at relevant points in any presentation or talk, is vitally important.

If you recall former British Prime Minister Tony Blair's way of speaking, you are likely to remember that he paused at seemingly inappropriate moments during his speeches, giving the impression that he didn't know what he was going to say next, or that he didn't know what he was talking about. So use pauses with care, but do use them.

Pauses allow your audience to take in the information you have just mentioned. Audience members can reflect and relate your content to their own experiences. And pauses also give sense and meaning to your presentation.

Don't tell your audience what you are missing out

All too often I hear people apologise during their presentation for running out of time and having to leave something out. As a member of the audience I feel short-changed. The speaker should have prepared better, allowed time for diversions and given us all they had planned. For me, it mars the talk and I leave feeling I missed something.

Yet what if the speaker had missed something out, but not told me? Then I don't know about it, so I don't feel short-changed.

So if you are running out of time and need to drop a section of your planned talk, or if you forget to mention something during your presentation, there is usually no need to tell your audience.

It is far better just to leave out the section and say something to your audience along the lines of:

I've given you the key points. There's a lot more I could tell you on this subject and anyone who would like to know more please get in touch . . . here's my email . . . or see me for a chat afterwards.

Introducing ethos, pathos and logos

In a book on presentation skills, inevitably the art of influencing crops up. Here I'd like to briefly introduce you to a three-step process from Aristotle and *The Art of Rhetoric,* which is still highly relevant today and regrettably not used often enough. For more detail on influencing skills see *The Influence Workout,* another book in this series.

When aiming to influence or persuade someone, it is often the logical argument that is thought to sway the decision. If humans didn't have emotions that would probably be the case. But we do, and therefore we don't think logically all the time.

- **Ethos** – in the context of a presentation it is important for the speaker to have ethos. Ethos is the level of credibility in the eyes of the listeners. Why should they listen to you? What experience do you have? What is your reputation?

- **Pathos** – creating an empathic connection with your audience. This is best created either through asking questions, or making verbal guesses as to their feelings, reactions and emotions if you haven't been able to suss them out earlier. As I mentioned in **Step 2**, in the section 'Demonstrating empathy', Prime Minister David Cameron rushed to Scotland a week before the referendum on Scottish independence in 2014 to make an emotional appeal to the Scots. In his appeal he stated he would be heartbroken if the United Kingdom was broken up. That was a statement of his own emotions and probably did little to appeal to anyone else's emotions, regardless of the way they were inclined to vote. Some might have felt it lacked pathos.

- **Logos** – this is where the facts and figures must back up the rest of your argument. All too often, over-reliance is put on this part of the decision-making process. Logos is important, but most of the time decisions are swayed through pathos – the emotional appeal of your argument.

 It is your role as the speaker to make your presentation emotionally engaging, as well as factually correct.

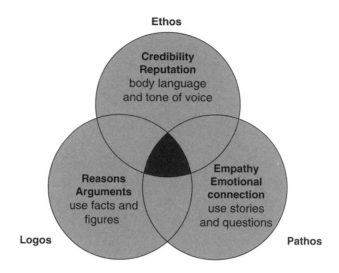

We make decisions based not on what we know, but on how we feel about what we know.

Case study

I can recall attending a workshop where the trainer said, *'I usually do this exercise, but in your case I'm not going to'*, without further explanation. Were we particularly poor learners, or especially good learners? Or perhaps he'd become bored with the exercise, or thought it wouldn't be well received? Or maybe he was running out of time? All these questions were generated in my mind, but if nothing had been said I would have been none the wiser.

Less would definitely have been more in this case.

 **Exercise**

Here are two exercises to help you improve the clarity of your presentation.

Take an article from a broadsheet newspaper, such as *The Times* or *Guardian*, and rewrite it using as few words as possible, but without losing any of the meaning and still keeping all the original facts. How many words were you able to cut out?

Here's a short extract from William Shakespeare's *Hamlet*. Try reading it aloud and see where you think the pauses need to be for it to make sense.

To be or not to be?
That is the question,
Whether 'tis nobler in the mind to suffer
The slings and arrows of outrageous fortune
Or to take arms against a sea of troubles
And by opposing end them

 See the online content for a short video showing different versions.

www.thebusinessgym.net

Call to action

- Reduce superfluous words and phrases.
- Avoid filler words.
- Know your main argument.
- Use ethos, pathos and logos to persuade.
- Don't tell your audience if you miss or forget something.

Step 8

How to handle questions

After reading this step you will be able to:
- Set the tone for questions
- Learn how to handle difficult questions
- Work with your chairperson.

The opportunity to take questions from the audience fills many speakers with dread. So far we have covered preparing a speech, crafting the words and using visual aids, but nothing about the skill of thinking on your feet to field questions and the unexpected. This step will take you through the myriad of situations you may find yourself in and provide you with guidance on how to handle questions and interruptions effectively.

Let's start with questions first

Before you begin your presentation you should decide what your question strategy will be. That way you can plan for questions. Essentially there are three options:

1. Take no questions at all.
2. Take questions at the end.
3. Take questions ad hoc throughout your presentation.

You may find the option is chosen for you depending on the type of event; for example, if there is a panel discussion then questions are nearly always taken at the end.

If you choose option one, to take no questions at all, there is no need to read this section further. But be aware you are missing out on a huge opportunity to get some valuable feedback into the thoughts your presentation has prompted in people's minds.

Formal events with a chairperson should already have a question strategy; ensure you ask what it is before you launch into your presentation. Hopefully, in that situation you will have a supportive chairperson who will help field questions, keep questioners on track and repeat the question. However, not all chairpersons are effective, and most really appreciate a conversation with a speaker before the presentation starts. Usually, at events with a chairperson, the strategy is to take questions at the end. In this situation it is extremely important you don't allow your presentation to overrun into the time allowed for questions.

If questions are to come at the end of your presentation, then to avoid a long and potentially awkward silence before someone thinks of a question you can prime your chairperson or a member of the audience with a starter question. This doesn't need to be a question you have invented – it could be one that you glean during your pre-event discussions with participants, or from chatting to the audience before you start.

Whatever approach to questions you decide to take, do spend some time thinking about the things you *don't* want to be asked. It is likely one of those will crop up, so be prepared as to how you will answer. If it is a confidential company issue that you are not permitted to address then say so. Otherwise, prepare answers to the awkward questions – these may be to do with price, delivery timescales, supply chain issues or product reliability.

Personally I like the spontaneity that comes with handling questions during a presentation.

There are upsides and downsides to this approach. On the upside you have a more engaged audience and your topic and presentation can be adjusted based on the questions. The downside is that you can go off-track if you're not careful; you may be asked something tricky that you hadn't prepared for, and time may run away from you so that you are left shortening your planned presentation.

Tell your audience you will answer the questions if you are able to, but also set them up not to expect you to have every answer – but you can promise to find it out.

However, you can stay in control by using some simple phrases, such as:

- Let me answer that briefly, and I'm happy to talk to you in more depth afterwards . . .
- I'm happy to talk to you later about that as it's not directly relevant now . . .
- I'm coming to that in a bit, so can you hold on until then and ask me again if I haven't addressed it . . .

 Exercise

Write down some phrases that might work well for you if asked a tricky question.

Techniques for handling questions

As well as the information below, there is more about this in **Challenge 7** in **Part 3**.

Breathe

It may seem obvious, but when presented with a question, it is human nature to feel a little uncomfortable in the spotlight. The natural body response is to freeze, which stops the mind from working and the feeling of going blank falls upon you. A deep breath, coupled with some of the other strategies below, can get you out of this situation. It also provides you with oxygen to power your voice in readiness for answering the question.

Repeat back the question

If you are fielding questions alone, or if your chairperson hasn't repeated back the question, paraphrasing what has been asked gives you thinking time, and allows the rest of the audience to hear the question. (Sometimes if the questioners aren't using a microphone the rest of the audience are oblivious to what has been asked and are therefore lost while you give your answer.)

Take some thinking time

It is okay to pause and gather your thoughts for a few seconds before replying. Using phrases such as 'that's a really good question . . .', 'I'm glad you asked me that . . .', 'hmm, let me think . . .' will buy you a few seconds, and also prompt your brain to get out of 'freeze' mode and back into 'thinking' mode.

Be honest

If you haven't thought about the angle your questioner has raised, or if it is something you don't know the answer to, honesty is the best policy. If you have a difficult question you can delay your answer, but *only* if you return later to the person or team who asked it with a suitable response.

One at a time

Taking questions one at a time in person is quite easy as you can see people raise their hand or make eye contact. However, doing this on a conference call is much harder. You can ask people to say their name if they'd like to ask a question; if there is more than one response you can draw up a list and then invite them to speak. Say the name of the person you are adding to the questions list so that they know you've heard their request. If you're taking questions through an online conferencing facility, such as Webex, you will be able to see the questions as they are raised. Be sure to tell people that you will break for questions and invite them to add any more. It is useful for others if you say who has asked what question, if you have that information.

Now let's take a look at interruptions

Interruptions can obviously take the form of questions, but they can also be in many other forms. People entering or leaving the room can interrupt your flow. A mobile phone might ring. A piece of equipment might fail. I've experienced a table collapse, a flipchart fall down, a delegate fall off his chair (yes, really) and even had a ceiling collapse on the audience! I've also had people come into the room while I was in full flow and walk straight up to me to tell me something, rather than wait in the wings for a suitable pause.

I've nearly had a heart attack presenting in an upstairs room when someone strolled past a window in what seemed like mid-air (I hadn't realised that there was a raised walkway outside). A colleague of mine even had a participant have a real heart attack in the room, but thankfully all turned out well for the person concerned.

Techniques for handling interruptions

Acknowledge

Making a verbal acknowledgement helps put the audience at ease. Everyone can see or hear the interruption, so making a comment about it and then returning to your presentation allows the audience to put it behind them and return to listening.

Use humour

If you have the sort of mind that is quick to come up with humorous responses, they can really help to ease the tension. For instance, if you stumble over something on stage, you could make a joke about how you were always so useless with your feet that you were the one left standing in line at school after all the sports teams had been picked.

What to do with the heckler

I recently watched a comedy show where someone in the audience tried to heckle. The put-down was quick and swift. The comedian said, 'It's ok; I brought my own material, thank you,' and proceeded to carry on with the show.

At work such a put-down might not be appropriate. I can recall making a put-down very early on and feeling so uncomfortable about it afterwards that I resolved never to do it again. It's just not my style.

The following responses might be useful if you don't want to use put-downs:

- **'That point's coming up next'** – but do make sure you do address that point next, or the heckler may return.

- **'I'm glad you brought that up, let's take 2 minutes to address it now'** – giving a time limit allows you to call the discussion to a close promptly, rather than letting it dominate.

- **'Good point, I'll speak to you afterwards as there's not time here to address your concerns in detail'** – and be sure you do find the person concerned to address the issue.

 See the online content for more examples of how to handle questions:

www.thebusinessgym.net

Taking part in extempore, off the cuff speaking opportunities or competitions can be a good way to increase your skills in handling interruptions and questions. I was terrified when I took part in my first debate. Having only gone along to watch the competition, I was 'volunteered' as one team was a person short. Since then the nerves still arise, but each time less so, and my skills have gone up in proportion to my nerves going down.

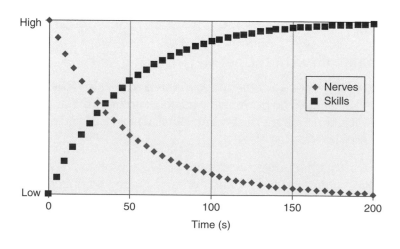

Case study

Dealing with a difficult participant

I was once in a situation where, on reflection, I think I should have asked the person to leave. I was running a workshop in London in the early evening. The person concerned constantly interjected comments, tried to take the session off topic, and generally became a nuisance not only to me, but also to others in the audience. It was a good many years ago and I was still new to running workshops. Initially I tried to answer his questions, then I changed tack so when he asked something I offered the opportunity to others to speak so that he didn't dominate. Finally I chose to ignore him and focus my energy on the other participants.

After the event ended I found out he had been out with clients for lunch and had continued to drink in the pub until it was time for the evening event. While it may explain the behaviour it doesn't excuse it, and if I'm ever faced with something like that again I would either ask the individual to leave or to at least keep quiet.

 Exercise

Review different styles of handling questions by watching three TV programmes, such as *Loose Women, Question Time, University Challenge, Oprah, The Jerry Springer Show,* or a news programme.

- What do you notice about the questioner's attitude, skill and the type of questions they ask?
- How does the recipient handle their answers?
- Who does or doesn't answer the actual question? How do you know?

Call to action

- Prepare in advance answers to questions you think the chairperson, organisation or audience might want to ask.
- Identify how much time there will be for questions, and honour the time.
- Repeat back the question so the audience can hear it.
- Don't be afraid to pause for thinking time.
- Address the questioner at the start of your answer.
- Keep your answers short.
- Be honest.

Step 9

How to deliver your presentation with confidence

After reading this step you will be able to:

- Find your confident self
- Present with power
- Stay authentic.

The biggest visual aid is you, the presenter. You are your presentation, not your slides. With that knowledge and pressure some people shy away from taking the limelight, while others are forced into it unwillingly. There are a few, but remarkably few, who relish the presentation slot from the outset. Most of us have to learn to manage ourselves and our nerves and develop our skills through practice, and along with that comes increased confidence.

If you are one of the lucky ones who has always relished making a presentation, may I suggest you do a quick self-check to ensure you haven't tipped over the scales into arrogance. Do you still consider your audience, do you still prepare, or do you opt to 'wing it' all the time?

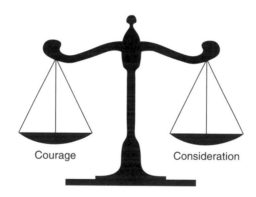

Courage   Consideration

As educator Stephen Covey points out in his bestseller, *The Seven Habits of Highly Successful People,* there is a balance needed between courage and consideration.

If you have lots of courage, but little consideration, the balance is uneven and tips into arrogance. It becomes all about you as the speaker and not about the audience.

Conversely, if you have too much consideration and little courage you spend your time thinking about what the audience want and not about the message you need to convey.

Keeping a good balance between the two helps to create inner confidence. You need to have courage and you need to consider your audience, but in roughly equal proportions.

A participant in one of my workshops once shared a lovely quote: *'There is room for humility in confidence, but not in arrogance.'* This step is for those who wish to develop their humble yet confident side. It will provide you with steps to increase your confidence when you need it, such as just before making a presentation, as well as strategies you can use at any time in many different situations.

Creating confidence starts before the day of your presentation. As you are crafting the words and rehearsing your presentation take notice of your self-talk. Listen to the subtle messages going on in your mind. Are they helpful or unhelpful?

For instance, we might say to ourselves:

- Why me? I don't know much about this subject.
- They've only asked me because no one else would do it.
- I hate making presentations.
- I'm no good at making presentations.
- It was awful the last time I gave a presentation.

 Add your own negative self-talk to the above list.

Can you counteract the negative thinking by replacing it with something positive, which will give your confidence a boost.

Your positive thoughts need to be realistic and relevant to your situation. These could be along the lines of:

- I've learned a lot since my last presentation and have practised this one a lot.
- I find making presentations challenging, but I know it will help me and my career in the long run.
- While I may not be the world expert, I do know what I'm talking about.
- I'm going to give it my best shot.

 Add your own positive self-talk.

For some people, replacing the negative with something positive works really well, while others find that their self-talk constantly works away, arguing against the positive thoughts. Keep in mind that this technique is not about arguing with yourself, nor is it about changing statements from black to white or true to untrue. It is a way of reminding yourself that the presentation can be viewed in a positive light as well as a negative one.

If this sort of positive thinking doesn't work for you, try one of the other techniques in this step.

Visualise success

Another confidence-boosting method is visualisation. Our brains have a natural tendency to focus on the negative, which means we can ruminate on what might go wrong until it creates a spiral of negative emotions in our mind. It is far better to run through strategies to deal with all the negative scenarios, to then leave your mind in a better place to focus on creating a positive scenario for your presentation.

In that way you are not hiding from reality; yes the PowerPoint might not work, you might trip up as you walk onto the stage, you might forget what to say. But with the correct preparation these events are less likely to bother you *if* they happen.

So rather than looking only at the negative, create your own positive version of how you want the presentation to be received, how smoothly you would like it to run and how well you will handle the questions afterwards. If negative thoughts start to crowd in on the process, try writing them down as this can help quieten them. If you do this the night before a presentation, you can fall asleep thinking positive thoughts. But don't let your positive thinking stop you from preparing; visualisation is no substitute for preparation!

Recognise past successes

Another technique to give yourself confidence is to recognise your past successes and use the positive emotions from those in the current situation. Creating a list of past achievements, however large or small, but significant in your eyes, and reviewing them before you give a presentation can bring the positive emotions to the fore. They don't have to be related to presentations either, just something you feel good about having achieved.

Role model

As well as monitoring your thoughts, visualising success and creating a list of past achievements you could try adopting the presentation style of someone you admire. Grow your confidence vicariously by assuming the persona of, say, chat show hosts such as Oprah Winfrey or Michael Parkinson, or perhaps someone in your organisation whom you admire. This doesn't mean you speak like them or use their mannerisms when you give your actual presentation. (However, you could do that during your practice sessions.) Simply imagine what they would do in your situation and then adapt that to your own natural style.

Stand tall

Your body language will speak volumes while you present. Make sure you remove any temptation to fiddle or grip onto the lectern or flipchart. Adopt a grounded stance, feet hip-width apart, with your weight equal on both feet, spine straight and with a smile on your face. To see the difference your thinking makes to your posture, do the exercise at the end of this step.

There is some research by non-verbal communications expert Michael Grinder on what makes charismatic leaders that he links to the use of a credible or approachable style, particularly pertaining to Western cultures. Grinder refers to these styles as 'Cats and Dogs'. Imagine how a cat acts, generally aloof and making contact when it wants something, whereas a dog is generally eager to please and is sociable. When making presentations the credible, cat-like style is one that has little movement, feet are planted, body and head are mainly static. This is a very useful stance to adopt when you are making a key point.

The opposite is the approachable style, that of the dog. This involves more bodily movement, nodding of the head and leaning forward with upward, outstretched gestures. This can be used to bring your audience with you on a journey and encourage them to connect with you and your content on an emotional level.

The best presenters use a mix of both styles according to the content and the reactions from the audience.

Don't be afraid of nerves

Once you have your posture and vocal tone congruent with your message your audience will hear what you mean them to hear, rather than a mixed message.

> *'I know you believe you understand what you think I said, but I am not sure you realise that what you heard is not what I meant'*

However, this doesn't mean your nerves needn't show and that you will be confident at all times. Actress Emma Watson made a speech to the UN on the HeForShe campaign. Her nerves can be heard in the tremor of her voice and she refers to them at one point, but they don't detract from her message. She is clearly confident and passionate about her subject (you'll find the link in the online content).

There is also more on handling your nerves in **Challenge 8** in **Part 3**.

Even high-profile people make a mess of a presentation now and then. Take, for example, Samsung's executive vice president, Joe Stinziano, as he invited movie director Michael Bay onto the stage at the Consumer Electronics Show to promote Samsung's new curved-screen TVs. Michael Bay found himself on stage without his planned autocue working. He attempted to start his presentation and stumbled badly. Joe Stinziano tried to encourage a conversation by asking, 'The curve? How do you think it's going to impact how viewers experience your movies?', but was met with a blank stare and a sudden apologetic exit from Bay. See **www.youtube.com/watch?v=R4rMy1iA268**

Case study

Don't emphasise your mistakes

When presenting at a conference for Women in Science and Engineering I wanted to use the flipchart. Pen in hand, I drew my point and then accidentally dropped the pen. Instead of picking it up I ignored it and left the pen on the floor. At the end of my talk in the Q&A I was asked how I had become such a good speaker: 'By not pointing out my mistakes,' I replied and picked up the pen and confessed.

A good speaker isn't perfect, but a good speaker knows what to draw the audience's attention to and what to ignore.

 **Exercise**

What does being confident feel like? Here is an exercise to demonstrate how confidence is linked to your thoughts and body posture. Read through the exercise first, and then put the book down so your hands are free.

 Or you can listen to this section and go through it via the digital content:

www.thebusinessgym.net

If you are able to, do this next exercise standing up. There are two situations to visualise.

First, imagine a time when things didn't go the way you wanted them to. It could be work-based or something at home. You don't need to tell anyone what it was; it was probably an unpleasant feeling. Where were you? Who were you with? What was being said? What were you saying? What could you see around you? Where is that unpleasant feeling in your body? Can you intensify it a little?

Now take notice of where your eyes have moved to, what has happened to your shoulders, where has tension crept in to your body, what has happened to your facial expression? Has your weight shifted from one leg to the other?

Then take a moment to shake out that feeling, wiggle your arms and legs.

Secondly, imagine a time when things went well, and you felt confident or happy. It could be work-based or something at home. You don't need to tell anyone what it was. Where were you? Who were you with? What was being said? What were you saying? What could you see around you? Where is that warm contented feeling in your body? Can you intensify it a little?

Now take notice of where your eyes have moved to, what has happened to your shoulders, where has tension moved to in your body, what has happened to your facial expression?

What is the difference between the first and second situations?

Most people notice that the first situation brings in hunched shoulders, tension in the jaw, throat or stomach (or maybe all three), eyes tend to be lowered and hands often move to be clasped in front of your groin, or arms become folded, your weight may be unevenly distributed between your legs, or you might even have crossed your legs at the ankles if you are standing up, and a frown creeps across your face.

In the second situation shoulders tend to be upright, as is the spine, there is less tension and often a lightness around the throat, heart or stomach area, eyes tend to be horizontal or raised, hands are often relaxed by the side of the body or, if clasped, they are not grasped but held lightly, weight is even between both feet and there may even be a smile on your face.

Having noticed the difference in your own body between the two scenarios, see what happens when you hold a confident posture and try to think of the first situation.

Stand with your feet hip-width apart, shoulders relaxed (draw your shoulder-blades backwards and down your back to do this), head lightly tilted upwards, eyes ahead or up slightly, spine straight and a big smile on your face. When in this posture hold it and think of the first situation, which was a time when things didn't go well for you.

Notice what your body wants to do.

Most people find that for their brain to access the first scenario the body desperately wants to move, the shoulders want to slip and the smile drops.

Now you have demonstrated how hard it is to think negatively with a positive body posture.

 There are more posture tips and examples online, but for now remember to bring your positive posture to any presentation and your negative thoughts can wait for another time.

www.thebusinessgym.net

Call to action

- Focus on the positive.
- Visualise success.
- Use positive body language (see **Step 6**).
- Remember that your nerves will be less apparent to the audience than they are to you.
- Be aware of your negative self-talk and try to counteract it.
- Don't hang onto the lectern, flipchart or props.

Step 10

Close powerfully and review your presentation

After reading this step you will be able to:

- End powerfully
- Make a call to action
- Review the effectiveness of your presentation.

You've reached the last step in **Part 1**, and if you've worked your way through the exercises you will now know the purpose of your presentation, have crafted your words and your opening, structured your content, decided how to use your visual aids, assessed how you will handle questions and got yourself ready to go with confidence.

Starting powerfully sets the tone for your talk. Crafting the words and guiding your listeners keeps them with you through your presentation. Here you will learn how to close powerfully, how to include your call to action and get the desired results from your presentation. In addition, there are some suggestions for reviewing your presentation and getting feedback, but for more suggestions on this approach see the mentor toolkit towards the end of this book.

While this step focuses on the importance of the close, to do this we need to return to the start of the presentation.

What was the purpose you set at the beginning? To tell, sell, impel or entertain? That will help you decide on how to close: with a call to action, to invite a purchase, ask for a meeting, encourage a change in behaviour or a rousing motivational message?

Some of the best presentations are ruined with a poor close. The close needs planning in as much detail as your opening. You need to know your intended close word for word. Rehearse, rehearse and rehearse again.

So how do you close?

Find a link back to your opening. If you had a theme during your talk, ensure you refer back to it at the end.

Let's take an example. Suppose you use the theme of trees as an analogy to growth: the acorn growing into the strong oak; strength coming from flexibility like saplings that bend with the wind; roots growing deep into the soil to provide a solid foundation. Your ending can't then be one that refers to rainbows as a vision of the future. You need to keep with your theme. Refer back to the acorn and the oak and encourage your audience to plant their own acorns, nurture them and grow the oak trees of the future.

 What analogies could you use?

Ask for what you want

If you have made a sales pitch, close with asking for the sale, or the next stage in your sales process. Making the call to action is often seen as the hardest part of a presentation, but remember the purpose of your presentation – if it is to make a sale you need to ask for the sale. Perhaps use something along the lines of 'you'd be delighted to have the opportunity to work with the business', or be more direct if that is your style and ask what more do they need to know before making a decision, or ask if they are now ready to place the order.

If you need volunteers to champion a project, you could ask for them to stand up or, better still, get everyone to stand up first and then ask for the volunteers.

If you are on a conference call, don't let it drift to an uncomfortable end. It is impossible to see that you have finished speaking, so be clear in your ending. Summarise the key points and say when the next call will be, if appropriate; then verbally indicate you have closed the call: 'Thank you all for your contributions to this discussion, I look forward to speaking to you next time, for now . . . goodbye.'

Don't say 'thank you' as your closing words

Be very wary of saying 'thank you' as your final words. By all means thank people for attending, for contributing or for listening, but don't let 'thank you' be the last words your audience hears. We have a natural tendency to remember the things we heard first and those we heard last, known as the primacy and recency effect. If 'thank you' are your very last words, you are missing a trick to make your presentation memorable. So if you need to thank people, do it before the end of the presentation and close with your key message or your call to action as your last words.

Don't undermine your core message with a last-minute thought

It is very easy to stray into ad libbing territory at the close of a presentation (as mentioned in **Step 3**). By this I mean the temptation to keep talking about 'just one more thing'. Keep to your planned close. Ad lib in the body of your presentation, react to the audience during your presentation and, unless there has been a total change of tone from the audience, stick to your planned ending.

When closing, close once. Deciding to add in another ending or a second call to action will dilute your original message.

Create a powerful ending

It is not just the words that create a powerful ending–tone of voice and posture are just as important. Practise the inflection needed for your close.

Go out with a bang, not a whimper

Too many presentations tail off at the end. The speaker is obviously relieved to have reached the close and their voice tails off. . . . Use vocal variety to go out with a bang, not a whimper. Indicate the close by being definite in your tone of voice and finish with high volume and energy and on a downward inflection in tone.

Pause for presence

As you near the end of your presentation, be very wary of the tendency to speed up your rate of speech. A closing message needs to be delivered with the same power as your opening. That means using pauses for emphasis.

Stand still

As you speak your closing words, stand still. You may, or may not, get a round of applause from your audience. If you do, *don't* rush to sit down as if the applause has acted like a pair scissors, cutting through the strings that bound you to the platform. You will appear far more confident if you stand still and smile as a thank you to your audience. As the applause dies down, then move to the side or to your seat.

 See the online content for some examples of effective closes:

www.thebusinessgym.net

Gathering feedback

You may have plenty of opportunity to get feedback from people after your presentation, but those you ask afterwards will probably be giving you their emotional reaction to what you said. This is fine, but often it doesn't help you improve. Someone saying 'it was good' or 'it moved me' or 'I found it very interesting' doesn't tell you what you did to evoke those responses.

If you want to get some really useful feedback, prime someone to listen out for certain things before you give your presentation and ask them for their detailed feedback afterwards. This may mean arranging a feedback meeting to discuss your presentation.

Make a list of things you want feedback about and prioritise them for the person who will be watching you. Ask them to look out for what went well *and* why, and what you could do differently or better *and* how.

When I am giving feedback, here are some of the areas I look out for:

- **Opening** – was the purpose of the talk clear? How was it established?
- **Content** – what research, evidence or facts were used to back up statements?
- **Structure** – how did the talk develop, what signposts or links were used?
- **Impact** – how confident did the presenter seem? Why? How did they engage the audience?

- **Close** – was there a call to action, or a definite close? How effective was it?
- **Use of voice** – pitch, pace, volume, emphasis, variety.
- **Use of language** – was it descriptive, grammatically correct, use of jargon, humour, triads.
- **Use of body language** – were hand gestures and body movements appropriate or distracting? What facial expressions were used? How much eye contact was made with the audience?
- **PowerPoint or props** – if used, how effective were they in backing up the message?

Don't ask someone to look out for all of these areas in one talk. Pick two or three key things, tell them what you are trying to achieve and ask them to evaluate whether you succeeded or not. Ask them to take notes and provide you with some specific examples if you are not recording your presentation.

Evaluation questionnaires

A lot of workshops are followed by evaluation questionnaires. These give information on the immediate reaction of the people present to the topic, the presenter's style, the venue and other questions that are included. But what you really want to know is, 'did it make a difference?' The only way that can be assessed is in the future behaviour of those who attended. Immediate feedback is often not the most useful.

The use of online questionnaires, such as Survey Monkey, is now more common to gather feedback after a presentation, especially formal ones. If you know a questionnaire will be sent out after your presentation you could ask for certain questions to be included, such as 'What are your three takeaways from this presentation?'. This will provide you with some insight into the key messages your audience heard. Then you can assess whether they were the ones you wanted them to hear.

Case study

This example shows how easy it is to detract from your core message by ad libbing.

I had been facilitating a company away day and the MD had been present and participated throughout the day. He had introduced it on a real high and the day had gone well. Yet when it came to the close he undermined one of the key messages of the day, autonomy. His words to encourage his senior team to be more autonomous were along the lines of: 'Be leaders, step up to the plate, be the dancing man on the hill or the first follower. . . and I'm sorry I haven't had much time to spend with you recently. I'll aim to do more in the future.'

 **Exercise**

Below are a few closes from famous speeches. Practise saying them aloud in your normal voice. Then repeat the exercise, this time using pauses, emphasis and inflection to create a powerful ending.

If possible, record yourself and listen to both styles. You will hear the difference that ending with power makes to the speech.

> *But I take up my task with buoyancy and hope. I feel sure that our cause will not be suffered to fail among men. At this time I feel entitled to claim the aid of all, and I say, 'come then, let us go forward together with our united strength'.*

Winston Churchill, Prime Minister of the United Kingdom 1940–45 and 1951–55

Note how Churchill avoided pleading for help.

> *Above all, we give thanks for the life of a woman I am so proud to be able to call my sister; the unique, the complex, the extraordinary and irreplaceable Diana whose beauty,*

both internal and external, will never be extinguished from our minds.

Earl Spencer, brother of Princess Diana, at her funeral

Note that he didn't say: 'Above all, we give thanks for my sister Diana who was unique, complex, extraordinary and irreplaceable.'

Now I want to say to you who think women cannot succeed, we have brought the government of England to this position, that it has to face this alternative; either women are to be killed or women are to have the vote. I ask American men in this meeting, what would you say if in your State you were faced with that alternative, that you must either kill them or give them their citizenship – women, many of whom you respect, women whom you know have lived useful lives, women whom you know, even if you do not know them personally, are animated with the highest motives, women who are in pursuit of liberty and the power to do useful public service? Well, there is only one answer to that alternative; there is only one way out of it, unless you are prepared to put back civilisation two or three generations; you must give those women the vote. Now that is the outcome of our civil war.

Suffragette Emmeline Pankhurst

Note that she didn't end by simply saying: 'There's no alternative, you must give women the vote.'

Call to action

- Link back to the start and the purpose of your presentation.
- Ask for what you want.
- End using a downward tone of voice, with high energy and volume.
- Close once, and close definitively.
- Slow down, pause and stand still.
- Avoid saying 'thank you' as your very last words.

10 presenting skills in action

This part focuses on providing specific tips for particular presentation situations that you might find yourself in. It is intended to be a reference guide, to dip in and out of as you see fit.

Presenting to sell a product

If selling a product is the purpose of your presentation, it is very easy to focus on all the good things your product offers and present these to make an apparently compelling case for your potential customer to say 'yes'. This is the most common mistake I see people make when presenting a sales pitch. All the positive information is downloaded in one long spiel, leaving the potential customer bamboozled and overwhelmed by lots of data, facts, figures and features of the product. When faced with this much information it is much easier to say 'no', or 'not yet', rather than ask detailed questions that risk another download of information.

To help avoid this pitfall, there are particular things to keep in mind. You will, of course, need to research your customer. (For more on this see **Step 2**, which covers understanding and connecting with your audience.) This skill looks at the following:

- Is there a downside to your product?
- The benefits of using 'but' to present the downside.
- Why you should not list all the features.
- How to make your product FAB.

Is there a downside?

First of all, does your product have a downside? Yes, strange as it may seem, I'm asking you to consider the negative features of your product. Why might your potential customer object to making a purchase? Maybe the product can be bought cheaper elsewhere, has a long lead time for production or doesn't meet the exact specifications.

If there is a downside your potential customer is likely to know it. They will be waiting to challenge you with that information. Marketing and psychology professor Robert Cialdini's work on influencing (www.influenceatwork.com) shows that it is better to present the downside first. His research has shown that presenting the problems first reinforces credibility and honesty. Be the first to include the downside in your presentation rather than wait for the customer to mention it.

The benefits of using 'but' to present the downside

L'Oréal use 'but' beautifully in their advertising strapline 'expensive, but you're worth it'. They admit their product is expensive. Cialdini's research has shown that following the downside with a 'but' helps to alleviate the issue psychologically. This is because 'but' tends to negate the words that precede it.

You might consider saying:

- 'It's a long lead time, but worth the wait for the bespoke product.'
- 'It's not the cheapest on the market, but it is (one of) the best.'
- 'It doesn't meet your exact specification, but it does ABC, which provides the same results.'

Don't list all the features, focus on the benefits

Having got the downside out of the way at the start of your presentation, you can focus on the sell. But don't tell your potential customer every single feature your product has to offer.

Why not? There are probably a large number you can list, and going through every one of them is going to bore your potential customer, at best. It is much better to ask the customer what they are interested in first and choose the features and specific benefits that relate to their situation.

The best way to make an effective sales pitch is to do your homework on the product *and* the customer. Make some guesses as to their needs, likely objections and the margin you can afford to give. On the day of the presentation, make it interactive by asking your potential customer what specifically they are looking for. What will they be using your widget for? What are the circumstances? What situations will the widget need to perform under, e.g. temperature, pressure, etc.? How many will they need?

By asking questions you will be able to decide which are the relevant features and benefits to mention. It will also engage your potential customer as they are involved in a discussion, not listening to you reel off a list.

Some questions to consider asking are:

- What problem is your potential customer encountering (which your product might solve)?
- How big is the problem? If it remains unsolved, what impact would that have?
- If your product could remove the problem, what benefit would arise?

How to make your product FAB

When running sales workshops in my past employed life, we used the mnemonic FAB to help identify whether and how a product would suit a customer:

- **F**eatures;
- **A**dvantages; and
- **B**enefits.

For example, a glass bottle may have many features:

Clear – advantage is you can see the contents

Size – advantage is capacity of one litre of liquid

Cap – screw-top lid, advantage is it's resealable

Label – advantage of being customised to the customer's requirements

Eco – made from recycled glass and advantage of being recyclable.

But if your customer has arthritis and is looking for something that won't break when dropped, then no matter how you pitch it, your product won't sell, because the customer cares about advantages and benefits to them, not the generic features.

 To sell your product, look at it from the customer's point of view.

 To understand the customer's needs, ask questions.

Skill **2**

Presenting a concept or idea

The challenge with presenting a concept or an idea is that these things are intangible; there is nothing for people to see, to take hold of or to smell.

The first consideration when making the intangible accessible to the listener is to use examples to bring your idea to life. Find stories, similar situations or universal experiences that can make it real and accessible in the mind of the listener.

Using stories

Stories are a great way of accessing people's emotions. They bring situations into the heart and away from the head; indeed, the heart is often where decisions are made, which are then backed up by the head.

I wonder how many readers will remember the days before YouTube, before CDs, before Dropbox, when information was shared through cassette tapes. Have you ever experienced the frustration of not being able to skip through the tape to the part you wanted to listen to? In those days you had to wind your way through the cassette, not knowing where the key information was – there was no easy way to skip to the interesting sections. Sometimes the tapes would get tangled by the player and be unusable.

You will, I'm sure, have watched a video on YouTube. You can see how long it is; at a click you can jump sections; and you can watch it again and again should you so choose, without having to rewind the cassette.

In business, life is sometimes more like the cassette than YouTube. Sometimes you don't know where you are, how people will respond or which bits will be interesting. You often have to go through the whole process to find out.

I have a collection of cassette tapes on the shelves at home from a story-theatre workshop by Doug Stevenson, creator of the Story Theatre Method for storytelling in business. This was in the days before YouTube and CDs. But thanks to modern technology you will be able to watch Doug give a taster of his storytelling skills by clicking on **www.youtube.com/watch?v=YUYyaXFO0FY** and listening to the benefits of hiding a pill in the peanut butter!

Similar situations

If you've watched the video clip in the link above you will know that Doug starts by using a question to establish a connection with his audience by asking about a similar situation: 'Who here has ever had . . . (in this case a pet who got sick)?' After telling the story he then makes the link to the business situation. There is no benefit to creating stories or similar situations if you don't create a link to the core message of your presentation.

What are the similar situations your audience could find themselves in?

Getting soaked in the rain . . .

Learning to ride a bike . . .

Slipping on ice . . .

Sun bathing . . .

How can that help you to make your concept or idea tangible, rather than conceptual?

Don't 'we' all over your presentation

I have discussed the benefits of using 'we' rather than 'I' to acknowledge the contributions of others (in **Step 3**), but there will be times in your presentation when it is better to use 'I' to emphasise ownership of the subject, statement or proposal. Showing personal commitment in this way can help generate confidence in the audience.

A picture speaks a thousand words

Sometimes when presenting a concept or an idea you need a visual to help the explanation.

I remember watching an architect speak at length about his amazing house designs and their energy-saving benefits. But it wasn't until he actually showed pictures of some built examples of his work that his presentation came to life.

What visuals can you use to help people understand and grasp what you want to convey?

Presenting to motivate and inspire

If you are seeking to motivate and inspire your listeners, I'm guessing you may also be looking for them to take some action: perhaps respond quicker to customers, work well towards a tight deadline or boost morale so that fewer complaints happen. Whatever the final outcome you are seeking, presenting to motivate and inspire is a huge challenge if you are not motivated or inspired yourself.

Use of fear

You've probably all been motivated by fear at some point. Possibly by a manager (I can certainly recall one such person in my corporate life who used to bawl at someone at random, and we were never sure when it would be our turn). Possibly the fear related to the consequences of missing a deadline or losing an account. However, while the use of fear to motivate may work occasionally, it isn't a lasting motivator, nor does it generate a flourishing environment in which to work.

Here is one example to illustrate 'away from' motivation:

The fire alarm goes off at work; you rise from your chair and make your way quickly to the nearest exit. Once safely outside you stop, start to mill around and chat with others. The motivation has gone and you wait until you can safely re-enter the building. You are not motivated to continue walking and go for a 10-mile trek. Why not? The fear stimulus has subsided and the reason for walking has gone.

Lasting motivation comes from the inside

It is not about finding an external key with which to unlock others, or kicking them into action, or even offering the proverbial carrot. Lasting motivation comes from the inside, from the values and beliefs of the individual, and is demonstrated though their actions. So how can you access it?

Motivating or inspiring from the inside

To really motivate or inspire someone you need to touch their inner emotions. In a presentation format, I suggest you use compelling stories, create emotional links and invite rather than tell your listeners to take action.

Storytelling

There is great power in using metaphors and stories to get your point across rather than directly telling (see **Step 5**). Human beings have a natural tendency to resist doing as they are told – just watch any four-year-old child. As adults we still have that four-year-old's response within us, even though on a day-to-day basis we supress the socially unacceptable response of 'no, I don't want to' that bubbles up inside us.

Using stories can give us a way to bubble up emotions in our listeners.

Creating emotional links

Aristotle knew the power of emotional connections and stories. While he could see that logical argument alone *should* persuade others, he was wise enough to understand that it didn't.

In *The Art of Rhetoric,* Aristotle proposed three steps that need to be in place to construct persuasive argument: ethos, pathos and logos (these are also mentioned in **Step 7**).

- **Ethos** is your credibility *in your audience's eyes*; why should people listen to you and why should they believe what you say? Often this is based on the reputation of the speaker, not the job title.

- **Pathos** is the emotional connection you make with your audience during your presentation.
- **Logos** is the logical argument, the facts and figures, the data and the reasons that back up your ideas.

The use of pathos in a presentation

Advertisers know these three steps well. They also know that the most persuasive, motivational or inspirational step is pathos. If you watch a TV advert you will often find it is selling an emotion rather than the product's features. Advertising agencies often use this technique in car adverts, but it is also used for many other products. And it works.

So find ways you can incorporate a link to the emotions of your audience. You might start with where they are now, then tell them where you want them to be, describe the difference, return back to where they are now several times during your presentation, before ending on where you want them to be and why it will be great when they get there.

Invite versus tell

If you invite someone to come on a journey, they have the right to refuse. In the same way, in a presentation if you invite people to come along with you they have the right to refuse. Equally, they have the choice to accept your invitation – and most people will do so. However, if you tell people they are to go on a particular journey, you may find you hit more resistance. A tell method of communication tends to butt up against the ego of the listener.

This can be demonstrated through the martial art of Aikido, which I have begun to practise. If, as a 'victim', we resist an attacker's approach and try to force them to the ground they, in turn, will resist and the strongest will win. However, a skilled Aikido practitioner will accept the energy of the attacker and use it to invite the attacker to come along towards the ground, and as if by magic they fall. (I am as yet far from skilled in Aikido!)

If you genuinely want to motivate and inspire others don't tell them what to do, unless you really have to – such as to prevent a commercially wrong decision being taken, or when the fire alarm sounds. Use the language of invitation and you will encounter less resistance and increase motivation and inspiration, and boost agreement with your views.

Metaphors

Step 5 provided some examples of the use of metaphors. Listen out for metaphors in everyday situations . . . the English language is prone to using metaphors and similes to express meaning, for instance:

- She didn't seemed bothered, it was like water off a duck's back.
- He took to the new process like a duck to water.
- She had an idea she wouldn't let go of, like a dog with a bone.
- You can lead a horse to water but you can't make it drink.

Is high energy essential?

It is often thought that the most motivational speakers are those with the highest energy. This might be a fair conclusion if you confined your search to America. There, speakers such as life coach and motivational speaker Anthony Robbins use big gestures, a loud voice, large emotional mood swings and bounce around on stage a little like Tigger in a sweet shop.

However, other speakers, such as the Dalai Lama, use their energy in a very different way. They are passionate about their topic, but present in a quiet, self-assured way.

To motivate and inspire others, you don't need high energy but you do need to be passionate about your subject. You do need to make eye contact. You do need to gesture, but in a manner appropriate to the topic. And you do need to be congruent with your own natural style – and be authentic.

Skill **4**

Presenting change

Why is it that when a presentation about a change in the processes, staff structure or procedures of an organisation is made it is often met with indifference at best, hostility or a passive–aggressive approach at worst?

How many times have you listened to someone presenting information on a forthcoming change and heard how great it will be without any recognition of the disruption the change will cause, the emotional feelings the audience might have towards the change or the reasons why it is being implemented?

Change presentations are often poorly received because they aim to put the change into a good light without any acknowledgement of the issues the change process will bring.

Not everyone likes change; only about 10% of people like things to be different year on year. Most people, 55%, prefer things to stay the same[1] (from NLP world www.nlpworld.co.uk/nlp-glossary/m/metaprograms/).

When presenting change, however positive a move you think it is going to be, you must recognise that not everyone will see it that way. Yes, present the positives, but only after you have acknowledged the resistance, objections and emotions your audience may be feeling.

If you use the word 'may', you are not telling your audience to feel a certain way, you are acknowledging what might be. For example, 'Some of you may be feeling a little frustrated or are thinking "here we go again" ... while others may be wanting to stop having to ....'

[1] NLP World, www.nlpworld.co.uk/nlp-glossary/m/metaprograms

Before making your presentation, brainstorm what is going to stay the same. That way you can present the change with sameness and difference in mind, rather than just difference. For instance, staff might:

- still be working at XYZ company;
- still be coming to the same office with the same colleagues;
- still have the same computer system.

Don't ignore the elephant

As discussed above, it can be very tempting to present change in a wholly positive light without acknowledging the negatives. It may be the upheaval, extra training or additional hours to be worked to get used to the change, or a reduction in hours and overtime as the new process will be faster than the old. Whatever it is, acknowledge it. If you ignore these issues during your presentation it will be like having an elephant enter into the corner of the room; everyone sees it and no one mentions it. The elephant will not go away, so greet it warmly, discuss it and then deal with it. Only then can the change be effective.

**"I suppose I'll be the one
to mention the elephant in the room."**

Use pathos

When presenting change, be sure to include pathos (see also **Step 7**). Too many change presentations focus on the logical argument, the reasons why the change is necessary, who will be involved and the timescale and process. While all that does of course need to be included, you won't get the buy-in until you use pathos to engage your audience's emotions, not just their logic.

It might be worth having a quick reread of **Step 7** before planning your change presentation.

Where are you and where are they?

Finally, as the presenter of the change you will have had time to think about the process, the impact, the benefits and the drawbacks. Remember, when you present the change it is possible that your words could be the first people will have heard about it.

Taking the 'change curve', attributed to and adapted from psychiatrist Elisabeth Kübler-Ross and her work on bereavement, it is likely you will already have moved through denial and anger to commitment, whereas your audience may well be in denial. Denial, with the emotions of shock or anger, is usually the initial reaction to change. Very few people greet change with glee at first.

Upon understanding a little more about the change, and realising it is going to happen, people may move onto the resistance phase. Here it is common to think that it will happen to others but won't apply to them, or that they absolutely will *not* use the new system or process.

Exploration starts when people ask questions such as 'how will that apply to me?', 'what is the impact of it on the team?' and 'why is the company doing this?'.

Commitment is the 'right, let's get on and do this' phase.

Often, as the presenter, you have had a chance to move through the first three of these four stages and are at least at the stage of exploration, if not commitment. There is, therefore, a mismatch between your emotional state and that of your audience, who may be back in denial or resistance. Be prepared to acknowledge this in your presentation and reflect on the stages you have gone through, articulating those to your listeners.

Presenting a team brief

How you currently conduct your team briefs, or indeed whether you have one at all, will affect which of the tips below are appropriate for you. As you read through this skill, keep your team in mind, the characters in the team and its objectives from the business point of view. Then choose which tip(s) to try out and decide which one to start with. Making radical changes may work, or you might decide to make them incrementally.

The purpose?

What is the purpose of your team brief? Is it to ensure that everyone updates each other on their current projects, or so that everyone hears the same corporate message at the same time? Be clear on the purpose or you may find you have more than one meeting muddled into a format that is contained within an hour on Monday mornings. Would it be better to separate your meetings into two shorter ones?

Engaging the team

A team brief can often be seen by the team as simply an information-giving exercise. If this is the case, why are you meeting up? Usually more is wanted from the brief, but not always obtained, such as a gathering of viewpoints, discussions or decisions. To achieve these extras the team needs to be engaged.

Sharing the chairing of the team brief can help increase engagement, as can using some of the facilitation tips described in **Part 3**. But perhaps the biggest tip of all here is to ask the team what they want. Your team will have ideas of their own; they will know what is working and what isn't. If you can draw those out and agree on what will be implemented, you will increase engagement far more than if you decide on your own, as the team leader, the format of future team briefs.

How long?

Some of the team briefs I attended in my time as a corporate employee lasted for up to 2 hours. Two hours every week is a lot of time out, and it wasn't always productive. Occasionally we would have a really useful session discussing a new product and how it would benefit our customers. But most of the time we were bored.

Short and sweet

Attention spans are getting shorter according to scientists. Keep the briefs short, to the point and then the content will be more memorable.

Stand-up meetings

Hold stand-up meetings rather than sitting down in a meeting room. One of the most useful briefings I used to have with a boss was every morning, for around 10 minutes, as we opened the day's post. That was before the advent of emails, and it gave us a chance to chat through the day, staffing and any other issues that were arising before I went to my team. We always stood up to talk.

Hold stand up meetings

Have an agenda

Even if it is a reoccurring weekly meeting, such as the team brief, there should be a purpose and an agenda, preferably circulated to everyone in advance of the meeting.

Start and end on time

Too many meetings don't start on time, usually because someone isn't present. Begin your briefing when you say you will and people will soon learn that they need to be there for the start. If you decide to wait until everyone is present, you will find the actual start time moves away from the scheduled start time and keeps moving . . . in the wrong direction.

Don't read the brief

One company I have worked with sends out daily updates and weekly briefs to their staff by email. The team leaders and the team receive the updates and these form the basis of the team brief. Unfortunately, some team leaders resorted to the easy option – reading out the email. Imagine the engagement of their staff at those meetings. If this is your company format, find a way to raise discussions based on points in the email; don't just read out the email as your team can do that on their own.

Identify the key areas

What is really essential for your team to know?

Can you describe the key points in 5 minutes or fewer?

Separate the 'must know' from the 'nice to know'.

Extra information

Holding shorter, more focused briefings means you won't be able to cover everything in detail at the time. So be sure to direct your team members to where they can find out that extra bit of information.

The middle manager's dilemma

Being a middle manager and presenting a team brief can pose an extra dilemma: how to pitch the message. Are you at one with senior management or are you 'one of the troops'. You will need to reflect both points of view, which can be a delicate balancing act. One thing that can help is to translate the language of a briefing out of management-speak or jargon and into the colloquial language of your team, so that they can relate to it more easily. As a middle manager with feet in both camps, you should be well placed to do this.

Own the message

This is especially important if a brief is likely to be controversial. Your team will see through the façade if you try to present a viewpoint you don't agree with. To get around this dilemma, you need to demonstrate that you understand the reasons behind the message. Then it is possible to say that while you don't fully agree, you do see why it is so, and you can ask your team to follow your lead in complying with the brief without undermining your own integrity.

Focus

Finally, when you are presenting a team brief, keep people on topic. Avoid a moan-fest. Allow and encourage constructive disagreement, but not moaning, destructive or vindictive language or viewpoints. See **Challenge 6** for more details on how to handle people with a persistently negative viewpoint.

Presenting a new project

While I know a lot about making presentations, I know less about project management. So this section has been written with the generous help of Keith Abbott, an expert in project and programme management.

When preparing your presentation consider the feasibility of the project, as you will probably need to answer the following questions:

- Is the proposal consistent with the company strategy?
- Does a market exist?
- Is the proposition technically feasible?
- Is the proposition commercially viable?
- What is the plan and resource estimates to deliver?
- What are the risks?

Often projects will have:

- a sponsor;
- an owner;
- a project manager;
- a project team;
- project stakeholders.

Key stakeholders usually include the sponsor, the project manager, the organisation and the customer. There are also other categories of project stakeholders, such as internal, external, suppliers and contractors, government agencies or society at large. Managing stakeholder expectations is one of the major challenges of project management, because stakeholders often have very different objectives that may come into conflict with one another. In your presentation, rather than ignoring the potential conflicts, acknowledge them and, depending on the time available and purpose of your presentation, it may be useful to open this up to discussion and input from those present to help address and manage the conflicts.

When presenting a new project you will need to create and deliver a clear statement of the aims, enabling the following questions to be answered:

- Is this in line with business objectives?
- What have we got to achieve?
- How will we know when we have finished?
- How will we know that we have done well?
- When has the project got to complete the tasks?
- How much will the project cost?

You may also need to include the following:

- **Project scope** – the scope defines and clarifies the boundaries within which the objectives of the project will be met, to ensure it is working to achievable limits. It may also, by way of further clarification, help to identify those areas that are out of scope.
- **Work breakdown structure** – the WBS is the basis for the project plan and needs to be reviewed in some detail at the kick-off meeting.

Project organisation and resource requirements

The management structure and organisation of the project must be clearly defined. Resources required to run the project must also be identified and a commitment obtained that they will be provided.

Initial cost estimates

Identify the initial cost estimates before the kick-off meeting so they can be collated and discussed at the meeting. If cost estimates are not available before the kick-off meeting, they should be derived as far as possible during the meeting and actions assigned so that the full costs can be included in the project scope definition document. The level of confidence in the accuracy of the estimates needs to be stated.

Milestones and major deliverables

A list of major project deliverables and target milestone dates should be presented and reviewed at the kick-off meeting.

Management system

Identify and articulate the management system. This helps to ensure that things go to plan, stating how the project will be reviewed, how risks, issues and problems will be managed, and how changes will be controlled.

Assumptions, constraints and dependencies

Any assumption, constraint or dependency should be identified and its impact understood. External dependencies should be identified and actions put in place with the owning functions to underpin the dependency.

Risks

A list of risks to the success of the project need to be drawn up, along with a plan to mitigate the effect of the risks should they occur. Generally, each risk will be assigned an owner who must assess the risk and develop mitigation plans. This list forms the basis of the risk register.

Immediate issues and actions

A list of immediate issues will have emerged during the discussion. As the presenter, it is useful to summarise them at the end, identify what needs to be done to resolve them and list any other actions.

Focus on needs

Successful presentations start by focusing on the audience's needs, and that also holds true for successful project presentations. Refer back to **Step 2** for a reminder on how to do this.

Presenting at a meeting

When making a presentation at a meeting, how formal you choose to make it will depend upon the nature of the meeting. For instance, if there are just four people present, a stand-up presentation with a full slide show may be overkill.

First of all, I suggest you refer back to the questions raised earlier (in **Step 1**):

- Why do you want to make a presentation?
- Is a presentation the appropriate way to get your message across?

Once you have decided that it is, and not simply opted for a presentation as a default method, then consider your audience, the situation and the message to determine the most appropriate style.

To use or not to use slides?

I recall being in a meeting at the end of the working day; I was with a colleague and we were pitching for a piece of work. My colleague had prepared a PowerPoint presentation and had copies of the slides printed and bound into a pack for each of the four people in the meeting. We had a brief discussion in the car park and decided that, as we were the last to present that day, the prospective client would already have heard more than enough PowerPoint presentations, so we would ditch the PowerPoint and talk them through the proposal in a more informal way.

This allowed the meeting to open into a discussion between the two of us and the prospective client, where they could ask us questions as they cropped up rather than feeling a need to wait until we had finished our presentation. Equally, it gave us an opportunity to ask them more questions so we could tailor our bid accordingly (and we got the contract).

Sit down or stand up?

When making a presentation in a meeting, if you need to establish your credibility and assert your authority you may find that standing up helps. Your body language is likely to be more assertive, and by standing you are in charge.

If you choose to sit down make sure you don't fall into the following traps:

- Don't slouch.
- Don't fiddle with your pen.
- Don't doodle.

- Do make eye contact.
- Do sit upright.
- Do lean forward.

Getting your point across

However informal the presentation, if it is going to be remembered you need to do your preparation. There is nothing worse than a meeting running over time because people have waffled, gone off on tangents and been unclear in their message (though sadly these are often failings of many meetings in business).

Be clear about your key message

Know what you want your audience to do, say, think or feel as a result of your presentation.

Be sure to summarise your key point at the end.

Getting heard

Often, in meetings, the challenge is finding air time. How do you get heard when everyone else is talking? Even if you are allotted a slot on the agenda, depending on the culture of your meetings this doesn't necessarily mean you will have silence while you speak. Maybe you don't want silence, as some interjection definitely shows engagement and listening is taking place; but I would suggest you don't want side conversations happening either.

If you observe a side conversation taking place, you could ignore it. However, a more effective option might be to stop talking, look at the people chatting and see if they look up. If after a few seconds, which may seem like minutes to you, they are still talking, as the presenter you have the right to interrupt them. Using their names to get their attention and asking if they have a point or a question that would be useful to share is one way of doing this.

Speak up

When giving a presentation in a meeting you will want to speak a little louder than you would if you were making a contribution to the meeting during a general discussion. Raising the volume slightly will help inject energy into your voice, ensure you breathe more deeply and provide an air of authority.

Where do you sit?

If you have a choice, take a seat where you can see the person chairing the meeting. You'll be able to make eye contact with them and enlist their support in controlling the meeting while you are speaking. When giving your presentation you do not have to do this from the place you have been seated. If there is an obvious front-of-the-room spot, get up and move there for the duration of your presentation. Choosing to present from your seated position might undermine your message, whereas choosing to get up and move demonstrates you are in control, both of the meeting at that time and also of your message.

Presenting on a conference call or webinar

When you know you will be presenting remotely, such as on a conference call or webinar, planning ahead of time is essential. Keeping people engaged is a bigger challenge when presenting remotely, so unless you are on a video call, you may need to prepare more slides rather than fewer. That way you can use the changing screen to help with engagement . . . but be sure to remember to move your slides on as you progress through your presentation. It is very easy to forget to do so.

The planning process has many similarities with those for the presentations already discussed. Here is a summary of some questions to consider:

- Why this topic?
- Why you?
- What might be the listeners' knowledge, skills and concerns?
- How can you make it interesting? Think of stories or examples of recent cases to include.
- What key messages do you want to get across? How can you highlight these?
- How long is it for? Can you chunk it into shorter webinars, or bring in guest speakers?
- Will you be asking virtual attendees to break out into groups for discussion?

Effective conference calls are well-chaired and allow everyone to speak without talking over each other. Having brief introductions at the start of the call so everyone can hear each other's voices will help identify the speakers if they are not well known to each other in the first place. As the presenter you will need to agree with the chairperson in advance whether you will be chairing the discussions on your presentation or whether they will be, and how this should be done.

Are they concentrating or bored?

Establishing a method of interjecting enables everyone to be heard. This could be as simple as saying your name to indicate you have a point you wish to raise. The chairperson then invites people to comment in order, by using the names. The chairperson will also know who hasn't raised a point and can then invite them to add their comments.

And regarding the technology, think about these questions beforehand:

- What equipment will you be using?
- Can you test it beforehand?
- Where is the mic located?
- Where is the camera located?
- If there is a technical issue how can you access assistance?
- Can you record a back-up presentation in advance?

Tips for presenting your next webinar

Don't

- Fiddle – either with your hair, a pen or anything else.
- Email at the same time as presenting.
- Have your phone on.
- Wear chunky watches or bangles that may clank on the desk.

Do

- Look directly at the camera.
- Have a strong opening, introducing yourself by name, and include housekeeping rules such as how to ask questions and where to write comments.
- Use pictures, including a photograph of you on the first slide to personalise your presentation.
- Introduce each speaker if you have guest speakers.
- Pause after you have made your main points.
- Avoid jargon and abbreviations – if they are necessary, explain them the first time they are used.
- Vary the pitch and pace of your delivery. This helps to keep the attention of your listeners and variety keeps brains attentive.
- Slow down your rate of speech; most of us unconsciously speed up when we make any form of presentation. The rate to aim for is between 140 and 160 words per minute.
- Pronounce the beginnings and ends of your words. This helps everyone clearly understand what you are saying and avoids mumbling.
- Summarise key sections and summarise key points at the end.
- Provide an overview of what comes next; for example, whether the webinar will be available as a podcast and, if so, how it can be accessed.

When presenting to a camera you have a choice of going up close and filling the frame or being further away. If you go for the up-close option, have some lighting positioned at 10 o'clock and 2 o'clock as it will help prevent you looking washed out. This isn't always possible, but do consider whether you are in the shadow or the glare.

If you decide to go for the further away option, be aware that your listeners may be looking at what else is in the room, who passes by the glass panel in the door or what is going on in the street – unless you can turn on a corporate backdrop as a screen.

If you decide to write out a script to read, ensure it is in colloquial language. We speak with far less grammar than we write. There are a number of autocue apps available, made especially for tablets, and these can make reading a script easier. Being too close to the camera when reading a script can show in your eye movement, so practise your reading distance. The further away you are, the less likely your eye movement will be noticed. If reading in a close-up position, try to keep your eyes on the same line (usually the top line) as the prompter scrolls.

Add in inflections, pauses and emphasis when reading. This should help to avoid your script appearing as if it is being read, and therefore potentially becoming boring to the listener.

Skill 9

Presenting data

When presenting data, the common trap is to put too much information on your slides, too much in your presentation and provide little explanation about what the data really tell the audience, why they need to know the information and what impact it could have.

I encourage you to join me on a mission to prevent poor data-rich presentations from happening.

Know your key message

If you can articulate why the data are important, what the information tells the audience and why they need to know it, you can start to plan a professional, clear, content-rich presentation. I say content-rich because that doesn't mean it has to be data-rich. The data needs to back up your message, but the audience don't have to have all the data given to them during the presentation.

If you refer back to the tips on presenting to sell a product **(see Skill 1)**, I introduced the concept of FAB:

- **F**eatures;
- **A**dvantages; and
- **B**enefits.

Perhaps, when looking at presentations containing data, it is appropriate to rename the concept DAB:

- **D**ata:
- **A**dvantages: and
- **B**enefits.

Ground your presentation in the data, but pick out some key points (advantages) that will be of particular interest to your audience and tell them the impact these will have, or the implications (benefits).

Craft your slides carefully

If you are using slides to present your data, do not, I repeat, do not put all your data onto the slides. I'm sure you can think of a presentation you've sat through where the presenter refers to the results of a survey, or a financial figure or a bit of technical information that is buried in the midst of the rest of the figures on the screen.

If there is an important piece of information for people to grasp, put it onto a separate slide, in *big* letters, yes I mean *big* . . .. Depending on the context, a size 64 font in Arial Black could work really well.

Watch out for nit-pickers

There is always someone who will spot the typo on your slide, a flaw in your data or challenge you on the statistical calculation you have used. Accept it; don't argue on your feet unless you are sure you are right and can conclude the point quickly. If necessary, have a separate conversation with the questioner about their point after you have finished your presentation.

Someone making a detailed or trivial point of this nature may be expressing a need have their ego 'stroked'. As a presenter it is your role to do the stroking, rather than lock into a battle of the egos. You may need to concede the pedant is right, or simply may be right. But telling them they are wrong and you are right will only inflame and prolong the situation.

Activities create understanding

During your presentation, can you ask your audience to take a moment to discuss the data with the person sitting next to them, in particular the key point of X and the implications they see . . . or something along those lines?

Having your audience do something active with the data, such as a task or discussion, enables them to understand the data more clearly, keeps the interest levels high and also provides an opportunity to generate questions.

Breakout groups can also be asked to manipulate or analyse the information and then come up with a recommendation for the way forward.

Less is more

You will already have seen this concept earlier (in **Step 7**) and it applies nowhere more so than when dealing with data. Make data interesting and less complex by distilling the key points. Use comparisons to generate interest, such as with competitors or past experiences.

Figures, tables and graphs

There are good and bad uses of figures, tables and graphs. I don't purport to say not to use them, but do use them sparingly. Create ones that, if you are showing them on a screen, will be readable from the back of the room. When presenting figures it is often more helpful to use percentages or fractions that the brain can relate to more easily. Give the detailed information on a hand-out, not in your presentation.

For an example of good and bad graphs, see the online content for more suggestions and refer to **Steps 4 and 6**.

Consider audience expertise

Take account of the expertise of your audience. If you don't know in advance what it will be, then assume a lower level of knowledge. You can always pitch your presentation higher, but if you have pitched it too high it is often difficult to think of on-the-spot examples to bring it to a lower technical level.

Are you presenting to accountants or engineers? What jargon will they be familiar with, what is industry-specific and what is product- or company-specific?

If in doubt, spell it out.

Presenting in 5 minutes

Making a 5-minute presentation should, on the face of it, be easy; after all, you don't have long to speak. However, the shorter your presentation is, the harder it can be to prepare and deliver an effective message.

When you need to keep it short, keep it simple

There isn't time for long explanations, long stories to illustrate your key points or lots of data on your slide presentation.

Take time to plan

Planning a 5-minute presentation can take longer than planning an hour-long presentation because you need to work out the essential messages and then show how you can present them in a straightforward yet engaging way.

Beginning, middle and end

In a short speech, even inside 2 minutes, there is still time to have a beginning, middle and an end. However, don't spend too long at the beginning with setting up the premise of your talk otherwise you won't have time left to cover the middle and the end effectively.

When giving short competition speeches of 2 minutes in length, I had to practise wrapping up my conclusion within 30 seconds. I still have a tendency to take a little longer than 30 seconds but the principle is there; a summary of what has been said and the key points *can* be made in a short amount of time . . . but you need to cut out the waffle. At the end you don't retell the message, you just cite the key points.

For example, when providing the weekly review of the team's progress, you could list all of the achievements and challenges you have encountered that week and the areas in which you are still seeking solutions.

If you have just 5 minutes I suggest you do the following:

- **Outline what you will cover:** 'This week I'll focus on one key achievement, two challenges and end with a request for help in the area of XYZ.'
- **Then provide the overview:** 'Our key achievement was in providing client A with their equipment on time and within budget. We have found challenges in the production line for product C and also in our night shift staff, as the team leader has been off sick. We overcame these by . . .

  Our remaining issue is that of the supply chain. To this end I am asking for your suggestions on how we might create closer links with them (and then open it up for a brief discussion).'
- **To close:** 'If anyone has further suggestions on the supply chain, please email or speak to me afterwards.' You could end there or add, if it hasn't been included earlier: 'In particular I'd like to thank Joseph and Jules for their perseverance in handling the challenges and congratulate the production team for achieving client A's timescale.'

The aim of a 5-minute presentation is to provide a quick overview, not an in-depth analysis. By all means state that you have conducted an in-depth analysis and give an overview of the results. Then point your audience to where they can find out more information, or provide it on a hand-out.

A word about PechaKucha

A different short-presentation format was devised in 2003 by the artists and architects Astrid Klein and Mark Dytham. Initially a way for young designers to meet, network and show their work in public, it has now become a recognised presentation format.

The name PechaKucha comes from the Japanese term for the sound of 'chit-chat', and the format is to deliver a presentation consisting of 20 images that change every 20 seconds. The whole presentation therefore lasts for 6 minutes and 40 seconds.

The rapid change of slides and short timeframe keeps people focused on the topic. There are now PechaKucha meet-ups all over the world, so if you would like to practise this format look one up: **www.pechakucha.org**.

Part 3

10 common presenting challenges

Challenge 1	How do I prepare with no time to prepare?
Challenge 2	How do I fit it all in, with little time available?
Challenge 3	How do I get people to listen and engage?
Challenge 4	How do I get people to take action?
Challenge 5	How do I manage interruptions?
Challenge 6	How do I manage difficult people?
Challenge 7	How do I deal with questions?
Challenge 8	How do I handle nerves?
Challenge 9	How do I remember what I want to say?
Challenge 10	How do I make a boring subject interesting?

This part covers 10 challenges that you may come across when making presentations. Don't scare yourself by thinking you will experience all of these every time you make a presentation. As you read the part, consider which are more likely to crop up when you make your own presentations. For example, some people know they will be presenting to challenging audiences, whereas others know that it is their own nerves that are more likely to be the challenge. Decide which is your challenge and head straight to it.

Challenge **1**

How do I prepare with no time to prepare?

Preparation can often be done before you know you will need it.

On several occasions I have met people who have complained about having had very little or no time to prepare a presentation. Yet, on questioning, it becomes apparent that they had known for a long time that a presentation was likely to be needed, but decided to wait until asked before giving it any thought.

The best way to prepare for a presentation is to give yourself plenty of thinking time. At each stage of working on a product or project, think how you might explain this to a customer or the board if you were asked to. Often you will find friends and family give you this preparation time accidentally by asking about your working day. If you stumble across a good explanation, jot it down at the time, otherwise you risk forgetting it.

So, aside from preparing in advance before you even know a presentation is required, how once you do know you have to give a presentation can you prepare with no warning, or very little time?

Let's consider the following scenarios:

1. **You are on your way to a meeting and in the corridor you learn that you have been 'volunteered' to present the project you are working on at the meeting.** Find three key points you wish to mention, jot them onto a piece of paper and stick to those. Offer to provide follow-up data to anyone who contacts you afterwards, or to circulate additional information as an attachment to the meeting minutes.

2. **You are in the meeting and are asked to give an overview of the project on the spot.** Take a deep breath (it gets oxygen

into your frontal lobes, allowing your brain to think). Thank the chairperson of the meeting for the opportunity to give your overview (buying you a little more thinking time).

Remember the basics of a presentation: to have a beginning, middle and end. Provide a bit of history, where you are at now, and where you intend the project to be in the future. Keep it short and offer time for questions. If you can, make three points in the middle section of your presentation.

Speak from the heart, not to impress, that way your passion for your work will shine through.

3. **You have a 5-minute warning before you are to present.** If you have 5 minutes or more to gather your thoughts and prepare a presentation then refer to the tips on structuring your presentation (see **Step 3**).

Personally, I find mind maps an excellent way of putting down my thoughts in a coherent fashion in a short space of time. However, they don't work for everyone. If you prefer to have your notes in a linear format, then highlight, asterisk or number your key points so you can find them at a glance.

Quick review

- Structure:
    - o beginning;
    - o middle;
    - o end.
- Use the power of three:
    - o Tell them what you are going to say.
    - o Tell them.
    - o Tell them what you have said.
- Start and end powerfully.
- Don't apologise for having not prepared, or draw attention to the fact that you were asked to make this presentation at short notice. The audience won't care about that; they care about what you have to say on your subject.

How do I fit it all in, with little time available?

Sometimes the challenge isn't having too little time to prepare, it is having too much time.

By too much time, I mean that you have had time to think of lots of things you want to include in your presentation, several different ways of getting your message across and a number of stories to illustrate your key points. The challenge then becomes one of squeezing it all in, which is never a good position to be in.

- Don't try and squeeze it all in, leave minor points out.
- Don't speak quickly so you can try and fit it in.
- Don't miss out pauses and emphasis because you are running short of time.

Sadly, I have seen many presentations ruin the key messages by clouding them with supplementary and unnecessary additional information, all because the speaker wanted to show all they knew on the subject.

Presentations are also spoiled by repeated mentioning of the lack of time and the amount of information that *could* be included, but isn't because there isn't enough time allowed.

Tips for fitting it all in

Working on the basis that the time allowed cannot be altered, you need to alter your presentation.

Here are three suggestions:

1. Decide your key points.
2. Don't tell your audience what they are missing.
3. Take your time, within the time available.

Decide your key points

Think about your presentation from the audience's point of view:

- What do they need to know?
- What are they particularly interested in?
- What objections or questions might they raise?

The answers to these questions will provide you with the key points you need to include in your presentation.

If you have time to elaborate, great. But it really isn't necessary. A short presentation can be just as, or more, impactful than a long one.

Don't tell your audience what they are missing

I have seen many good presentations damaged by phrases such as:

- I haven't got the time to go into detail here.
- Sorry, I'm going to have to skip over XYZ.
- I had hoped to be able to cover ABC, but I've run out of time.

Your audience ends up feeling short-changed because you haven't planned your presentation well enough for the time available. A tip I learned early on in my speaking career was not to mention time constraints. I also learned to plan an extra section that I could include if there was time available, and a section I could leave out if I ran out of time. Always be able to jump to your concluding points – and your conclusion should not have *anything* in it that you haven't mentioned in the body of your presentation.

If you want to provide extra information to your audience after the main presentation, that is absolutely fine. Just don't do it by way of an apology, or by telling them you haven't been able to include it. A good presenter will make it seem that it was planned to provide the extra detail in a different way all along. This could be by email, an online portal, a hand-out or other means that suit your business. Alternatively, keep that information until your next presentation.

See **Step 6** on best practices for PowerPoint, to show you how to skip slides without it being obvious to your audience.

Take your time, within the time available

However short the time is for your presentation, you won't succeed in getting your message both heard and understood if you speak too quickly. Take a look at the digital content and the information in **Step 7** on the rate of speech to help with slowing things down.

People need time to listen and reflect on the information: how does it apply to them and their situation? What are you asking them to do or say? Pauses, repetition and reflective questions can aid this process far better than cramming in extra information and running through it too quickly.

Challenge 3

How do I get people to listen and engage?

There may be a number of reasons why your audience are unresponsive or inattentive. Assuming it isn't your monotonous voice or poor slide presentation that is causing them to disengage from your presentation, there are some tips and techniques you can use to create more engagement and generate greater interaction.

First of all, you need to be engaged yourself, both with your material and the audience. However, coming across like a game show host, with overly enthusiastic encouragement, can turn some people off even more, so pace yourself to create rapport and draw the audience with you rather than starting at a high energy level they can't relate to.

Facilitate, don't present

While the focus of this book is on presentation skills, a good presenter will know when to present and when to change their style to a more facilitative approach. This provides a higher level of audience participation, discussions and interactions. However, it also provides opportunities to go over time or off topic, which needs careful management.

Despite the possible drawbacks, a facilitative approach definitely increases engagement.

Instead of giving someone a list or the facts, ask them what they know

One woman I was coaching needed to include some technical information in her presentation; in this example it was a set of rules defining the responsibilities of sellers and buyers for the delivery of goods in export markets. Her initial approach was to list all of the rules in her presentation, with their definitions. But that didn't take account of what her audience might already know, or at least be able to work out for themselves. Instead she started by asking the audience which rules they already knew. This created far more involvement and allowed her to focus on the particular rules that her audience were not familiar with, instead of boring them with information they already had.

Create a quiz

You could create a topic-based quiz, perhaps interspersed with some wider company facts or current media items. Add some prizes to get even more engagement: I find that chocolate works well!

Pause

People get used to hearing presenters drone on, and on and on. Putting pauses in your presentation provides opportunities for them to reflect on what you've said, relate it to their situation and work out what they might do with the information.

Invite discussion

Depending on the size of your group, you might want to ask people to break into small groups, speak to their neighbours or simply invite discussion with the whole audience . . . or a mix of all three during your presentation. Whatever approach you take, inviting discussion increases engagement with the topic, but doesn't guarantee agreement.

Use Post-its

I am hugely grateful to Arthur Fry and Spencer Silver for the invention of the Post-it note. Post-its allow comments to be collected, collated and sorted – often anonymously – in all sizes of groups.

If you use Post-its, be sure to reflect back the sentiments described in the Post-it comments in a plenary session, even if you don't read every Post-it aloud to the group.

Wave a flag

Not literally, but metaphorically. Use verbal language to flag up important points, to get people to sit up and take note, to engage and listen. Adopt phrases such as:

- 'Heads up...'
- 'This is a really important point...'
- 'If you take nothing else away from today, remember this...'
- 'The key point is...'
- 'To summarise...'
- 'To conclude...'

Ask questions

As I've mentioned in earlier sections of the book, the use of questions engages your audience. Use both rhetorical questions, with a pause to allow a little reflection time, as well as questions you are seeking an answer to.

Leave for a short while?

As the presenter, do you need to be there the whole time? If you are leading a team and want some honest feedback, sometimes it might be better if you leave the room, allow your team to have a discussion for, say, 5–10 minutes (tell them the timeframe) and then return to gather the feedback, perhaps on Post-it notes. Don't forget that if you are on a conference call or webinar it is still possible to break people into groups, depending on the technology you are using.

Advance priming

You can contact your audience in advance by telephone, circulating an agenda or emailing the key discussion topic. Ask them to submit questions or comments before the meeting and use these towards the beginning of your presentation – if you leave it too long people may start to wonder whether you have forgotten or dismissed the comments they made, which could create greater disengagement.

Use your sensory acuity and flexibility

Be flexible: what is it people are interested in? Listen to what is being said, and not said. Watch the body language. Adjust your style and content accordingly.

How do I get people to take action?

Have you given a presentation, come to a conclusion, had people nod in agreement and then do nothing. What happened?

For people to take action following a presentation they need to be:

- emotionally involved;
- accountable; and
- committed.

Emotionally involved

Generating emotional involvement is so important that it comes up throughout this book. But if you haven't read the other sections yet, here is a quick summary:

- **Use ethos, pathos and logos.** Ensure you focus on pathos and connect to the emotions of your listeners.
- **Tell stories.** Emotional involvement comes through effective storytelling, rather than presenting dry facts or information. Create a compelling case by telling stories. For instance, what is the current situation? Where will it be if nothing happens and where could it be if everyone takes action?

Accountable

It can be a useful trick to refer back to actions identified during a presentation at a later date, possibly without people expecting you to do so.

I recently facilitated a leadership team meeting for a large corporation and at the end everyone wrote their actions onto Post-it notes and shared their top action with the rest of the room. Four weeks after the event, each participant received a phone call from me, out of the blue, to ask how they were getting on with their actions and to ask for feedback about the event itself. I was pleased that many had actioned their commitments: one person was even moving his Post-it note forward every day in his diary to remind him of his ongoing action. The two people who hadn't done anything about their actions said they were grateful to be prompted to revisit their commitments. The actions were then followed up at the next leadership meeting.

An alternative to you as the presenter or manager holding people accountable is to create a buddy system in the room, where the members of your team hold each other accountable.

Another alternative is to get everyone to write their actions onto a postcard, with their address, collect them in and then send the postcards out around 3–4 weeks later (or longer if you think it's appropriate). One word of caution with using this approach – be sure that your listeners get to record their actions for themselves somewhere else, as well as on the postcard, otherwise they may justifiably use memory failure as a reason for not taking action until the postcard arrives!

Committed

Making a public statement can generate commitment. Research by Robert Cialdini shows that if people make a public commitment they are more likely to be consistent in their actions. So, rather than let people nod their way through your presentation, ask them to verbalise the actions they will take. That way you can discuss with them if their actions are off track, or just note down the actions if they are on track.

You could ask one or two members of your audience to capture the actions onto a flipchart. You can then photograph the flipchart and email the picture alongside the minutes of the presentation.

Minutes? Definitely ensure action points are noted at the time and circulated promptly after your presentation. Full-blown minutes might not be appropriate, but circulating the actions will be if you are expecting people to do something as a result of your presentation.

Hold a follow-up meeting

Holding a follow-up meeting to discuss the actions, or creating sub-groups to take the actions forward, keeps the ball rolling.

Enlist senior support

You might need to enlist support for the implementation of actions. Who do you need to communicate with (for example other people's managers) to make sure that people are not being pulled in different directions by different managers? This will also discourage people from using their own manager as an excuse for not taking action.

Identify resistors

As with anything, there are likely to be one, two or a few people who are natural resistors, especially to change. If you can identify who they are you can take steps, such as enlisting your early adopters to support and encourage them.

Rome wasn't built in a day

Sometimes the actions people intend to take are too big a step, too time-consuming or they have too many and don't know where to start, and therefore nothing happens. Remember, Rome wasn't built in a day: a change implementation or a culture shift doesn't happen overnight. It may be that you need to encourage more constructive confrontation, rather than agreement, for future decisions to be effective. If that sounds like your situation, I recommend that you get a copy of *Five Dysfunctions of a Team* by consultant and speaker Patrick Lencioni, where you will find lots of ideas on how to start making this happen. Over two million copies of Patrick's book have been sold, with good reason.

Challenge 5

How do I manage interruptions?

During presentations you need to be prepared for any unexpected events, and one of these is interruptions. They may come in several forms: the vocal interruption from someone interjecting their point of view; the visual interruption, such as seeing a flipchart slide from the wall, or someone walk in or out; or a noise interruption, such as an aeroplane passing or a crash of plates.

If it is someone in your audience interrupting your talk to make their point, then you have a few options:

- You can allow the interruption – after all it may be a valid point.
- You can thank the person and ask if you can take their comment at the end of the presentation.
- You can ignore the person and pretend you haven't heard them.

What you do will depend on your confidence, whether you know the person, whether the comment is on topic and how much time you have left.

To manage an interruption, be firm. Don't say, 'Would it be ok, if you don't mind, if you could possibly umm, er keep your comments until the end? Thank you.' Be firm and clear in both your vocal tone (keep it low), your verbal language (keep it clear and clean) and your body language (stand upright, be still and make eye contact). Say what you want to have happen and make your request firmly and politely. If the other person doesn't agree with you, see the next challenge about dealing with difficult people.

Examples of how to deal with the interruption effectively might include:

- 'Thank you Fred, you've made some very valid comments there. I'd like to discuss those at the end once everyone has had a chance to consider the rest of the information I'm about to present.'
- 'Thank you Fred, hold on to that thought and I'll come back to you at the end. Interrupt me again if I don't.'

If you have asked someone to wait until the end of your talk before taking their interruption, be sure to invite them to speak before you take any other questions. If you pass them over for someone else without at least an acknowledgement or reason why, they are likely to become agitated and may interrupt again.

Enlist support

Other people in your audience can be extremely useful in managing an interruption. After hearing the comment, passing it out with a 'what do the rest of you think?' allows your audience an opportunity to make a judgement as to whether the point is valid or not, without you needing to do so.

Keep calm and manage your emotions

Stay calm and be willing to forgo some of your own ego in order to stroke the other person's. They may simply wish to be seen as a big fish or a force to be reckoned with. The chances are others in the room will know the real story.

Interruptions can throw you off your train of thought. Take a breath after the interruption to gather your thoughts, and even vocalise to your audience something along the lines of 'right, let's carry on then. . . '.

I recently had to deal with two different situations where I was interrupted by someone walking into the room. The first was at a workshop that I was running on a client's premises. Part way through the morning the client's HR manager walked in, came straight up to me while I was in full flow, handed me a non-urgent message, turned and walked straight out, with not a word said. After she left the room, we all looked at each other and chuckled. I gave the participants a quick overview of the message and then carried on the workshop. The chuckle allowed us all to put the event behind us and move on.

The other interruption happened towards the end of a conference presentation when I suddenly felt someone standing silently by my right shoulder. I've no idea how long he had been there distracting the audience, waiting to tell me that I had 2 minutes left. After he walked out, I raised my eyebrows to acknowledge the unnecessary interruption and carried on. Again, it was the acknowledgement of the interruption that was important; don't leave that elephant in the room!

Visual interruptions

If the interruption is a visual one, I suggest acknowledging it only if other people have also seen it. If it is something you alone have spotted, you can choose to ignore it.

Noises

Most of the time I acknowledge noisy interruptions. This can be done in a humorous way if you can think of an appropriate retort on the spur of the moment, or simply a facial expression. This allows your audience to show a reaction to the noise and to return their attention to you and your presentation. If it remains unacknowledged, the chances are a few people will be wondering what the noise was or how much damage was done (in the case of dropped glasses or the equivalent). If it is a noisy aeroplane overhead, unless you are working at an airport where that type of interruption will be frequent (which I have done), I suggest you wait until the moment has passed before you continue with your presentation.

How do I manage difficult people?

What type of person do you consider to be difficult?

This question raises the whole issue of personality traits, behavioural signs and feelings. But, in essence, we are likely to consider a difficult person to be someone who is different from us. It is almost invariably that difference that causes the difficulty, rather than a deliberate intention to be difficult (although that cannot be ruled out).

Difficult people in the context of making a presentation are often those who take a different viewpoint and want it to be heard.

Who is difficult?

Can you find out who is likely to be difficult in advance of your presentation? If you are presenting to your team you will know the characters well enough, but if you are presenting to a group you haven't met before it is often useful to find out what differences of opinion you might encounter. Personally, I tend to avoid finding out exactly who the difficult people are going to be as I don't want to pre-judge their behaviour. But sometimes it is useful to know exactly who will be asking the most challenging questions or who will be the hardest to persuade.

Separate the behaviour from the person

If you see someone as being a 'difficult' person you will probably pick up on every little piece of their behaviour that doesn't back up you or your presentation and miss those that do. Human beings are very adept at selective attention, and once we have labelled someone we tend to fit their behaviour to that label. We focus on our preconceptions and can block out some very obvious contrary cues. (For fun, see this short video about selective attention: **www.youtube.com/ watch?feature=player_embedded&v=IGQmdoK_ZfY**)

So think about challenging behaviour, rather than difficult people. If you can work out the cause of the challenging behaviour – and there will be one – then you are part way to dealing with the behaviour itself.

Change your thinking

If you think a person will be difficult, the chances are that they will be, in your own mind at least, because of your selective attention. So change your thinking. Are they being difficult, or just asking difficult questions? Are the questions difficult or just ones you are not ready, willing or able to answer? Are they a lone thinker or asking what the rest of the group is thinking?

Acknowledge the intention behind the behaviour rather than labelling the person. Value their opinion; after all, they might be right and you might be wrong.

If they challenge some of the data you are presenting, might they have a point? You could concede their right to a difference of opinion and offer to investigate and get back to them afterwards.

The key is to acknowledge their viewpoint, not necessarily agree with it. By acknowledging it, rather than countering it with an 'I'm right, you're wrong' approach, you demonstrate you have heard them, really heard them. If you get into a discussion or argument on who is right you are likely to lose credibility as a speaker with the rest of the audience, and still not win over your difficult person. It becomes a battle of the egos, but as a presenter your focus should be on the audience and their egos, not yours.

Practise the art of *nemawashi*

Nemawashi in business is the art of influencing one person at a time to gain consensus (see **Step 2**) and can be useful if there is a person you suspect might be difficult. This involves meeting people one on one before your presentation to see what their views are, to gather information and to present your argument before going into the main meeting.

I recall needing to make a proposal to a board meeting where I knew that one particular individual was knowledgeable on the subject and might want to air his views at the meeting. So I contacted him in advance and asked him for his views on my proposal. He agreed with what I was putting forward and I went happily into the meeting knowing I had him on board. Or so I thought . . .. During the meeting he became increasingly vocal and appeared to be contradicting me. I realised that one of the mistakes I had made was to sit on the same side of the table as him, at the opposite end, so I couldn't make eye contact with him. I needed to find a way to look him in the eye when making my next point. So I moved my position slightly by reaching for a drink, took a deep breath, leaned forward a long way and looked down the table to make eye contact as I addressed him with the details and facts that we had agreed on in advance.

Points to remember about these individuals:

- Difficult or different?
- Identify them in advance.
- Speak to them in advance.
- Sit where you can make eye contact with them.
- Stand up to assert yourself if necessary.
- Pause your presentation and wait for them to calm down.
- Be prepared to ask them to leave, or mute them if you're on a conference call.

And above all:

- Stay calm and breathe.

How do I deal with questions?

Taking questions from the audience can be nerve-racking and does take a degree of confidence. Over the years I have developed an ability to respond on my feet, but it wasn't something that came naturally. For me personally, taking part in debating competitions and impromptu speaking competitions helped to develop this skill. But once you have it, it will also stand you in good stead in any form of meeting where you may be put on the spot.

So what are the key things to do?

There are some things you can do before you give your presentation to anticipate questions that you might receive. Think about who is going to be there, what they might want to know and what you don't want them to ask. Deciding what you don't want them to ask gives you a great start on what to prepare answers for, as you can be pretty sure that one of those difficult questions will crop up.

As you invite questions:

- Remember to breathe.
- Look people in the eye.
- Maintain your confident stance.

Tips for handling questions

Take one at a time

You may need to act as chairperson and indicate to someone that you have seen they want to ask a question, and perhaps even mouth to them that you will come to them next.

Repeat the question

Repeating or paraphrasing the question if you are unsure what the person said or meant enables you to check your understanding. It will also give your brain a little time to think of an answer, and provide those who didn't hear the question the chance to understand what you are answering.

Don't fudge

Answer the question as best you can or if you are unable to do so, say so. Don't fudge the issue. If you can't give an answer because it is confidential information, or needs sign-off before it becomes public, I suggest you say so.

Be honest

If you don't know the answer it is best to admit it. The key is to return to the questioner with the answer once you have found it out, or to point them in the right direction to find it themselves.

Tell your audience when to ask questions

I prefer to take questions during a presentation, if it is informal enough to allow that to be the case. You may find that puts you off track, so if you decide to go down this route, be sure to keep track of your thread.

Step into the audience

Be willing to step into the audience if the environment allows. For instance, small groups may be in a horseshoe shape that you can walk into or clusters where you can go round each table.

Check you have answered it

If necessary, check back with the questioner as to whether they are happy with your answer. Or if you know you haven't answered it, say so. For example, you might say something like:

That's probably not directly answered your question. I can't give you any more information at the moment, but do come and talk to me privately afterwards and I'll raise your concerns for you.

Facilitate the generation of questions

Split people into small groups to generate questions if you think they are unlikely to say anything aloud to the large group. This works particularly well when people might want to ask contentious questions and don't know whether, or how, to. If you appoint a spokesperson or ask for questions on Post-its, this can help prevent the questioner being identified and can elicit more in-depth questions. In addition, collecting questions on Post-its allows you to decide the order in which you take them, and you can group similarly themed questions together.

Challenge 8

How do I handle nerves?

Everybody is nervous when they make a presentation, unless you started making yours around the age of four, before you had learned to be nervous. People are born with innate fears, such as those of loud noises, falling and snakes. . . but four-year-olds don't have a fear of standing up in front of people and giving a presentation. That is learned behaviour.

So where did you learn your fear of speaking from?

Perhaps you were told by your parents not to show off, or you were the butt of jokes at school whenever you did something out of the ordinary, or maybe you gave your first presentation and froze, forgot what you wanted to say and slunk off the stage thinking, 'I am *never* going to do that again!'. Yet here you are, finding the need to give presentations as part of your job, and you can recall that feeling as if it was yesterday. Fortunately, most of us don't need to undergo extensive psychotherapy to uncover the root cause of this fear, as the issue is how to manage it, rather than where it came from.

However, for some people the fear of public speaking is so deep-seated and pervasive that it can affect their ability to function in everyday life. If this is the case for you, please discuss it with your GP as you may be experiencing an anxiety disorder that would benefit from specific treatment. Many options are now available for helping people overcome anxiety disorders, which are far more common than you might think.

As humans, we typically have a choice of three reactions to fear: fight, flight or freeze. Assuming you *have* to give your presentation, the fight or flight responses are less of an option; it is the freeze response, where your mind suddenly goes blank, that you need to be aware of.

Everyone has some level of nerves when giving a presentation, including me. For me, it seems to be down to caring too much about the outcome and what people will think of me. If I was truly complacent and didn't care, perhaps my nerves wouldn't be present, but then I would be performing at a lower level.

Tips for handling nerves

Accept the nerves

The first step is to accept the nerves; they show you care.

Forget trying to get it right or be perfect

You are human, and humans make mistakes. If you have read through the rest of this book and put in the preparation and practice you will have a good presentation to give, but there is no way that it will be 'perfect'. Accept that.

If you make a mistake, either embrace it or ignore it

My preferred option is to ignore mistakes rather than point them out. If you can see your audience really spotting it, such as a misspelling on the flipchart, acknowledge it and move on. Mistakes often go unnoticed by the audience and they will remain focused on the content unless you draw their attention to the error.

Breathe

Breathing deeply helps to slow your heart rate and gets blood to your frontal lobes to help you think more clearly.

Focus on your audience

Paul Dolan, professor of behavioural science, writes about his stammer in the introduction to his book *Happiness by Design*. He came to realise that the amount of attention he was paying to his speech compared to the attention paid by others was completely at odds. His stammer wasn't noticed by most people, but focusing on it made it worse. Once he stopped paying it so much attention it lessened in intensity. Where you focus your attention during your presentation matters; if you think 'I'm really nervous' or 'I'm going to mess this bit up' it will exacerbate your nerves and be unhelpful to your delivery. Instead, focus on your audience. When I'm giving a presentation I go into a different mindset, almost an altered state. It may sound odd, but I stop focusing on what I'm going to say and how I'm going to say it; that is something I have done before the presentation starts. I focus on my audience.

Widen your peripheral vision

Nerves and nervousness make our vision narrow. Widening your peripheral vision and focusing on what you can see out of the corner of your eyes before you begin your presentation can help to calm your nerves.

Use affirmations

Some people find repeating positive affirmations either out loud or in their heads really helpful. These could be 'I know my talk', 'I have prepared well', 'I am developing my skills as a presenter', 'I will do my best' or, if it works for you, 'I am a great presenter'.

Alter the negative

Human beings have a cognitive bias towards negative thinking. This is not helpful when giving your presentation, but can be very helpful during the preparation stage. When preparing, you can run through all the things that might go wrong and either take steps to prevent them from happening or decide how you will handle them if they do. As you get to the night before your presentation, stop the negative spiral and focus on the positive. Focus on what you want to have happen, how you want your audience to respond, imagine your presentation going smoothly, on time and with actions agreed at the end.

If you still have negative thoughts spinning around your head before a presentation, then do your best to rework them into something positive. Make them into a positive action, such as 'increasing skills set', 'learning how to present' or 'growing in confidence'.

Stay in the present during your presentation

Keep your mind focused on the here and now, rather than on the whats, ifs or maybes.

Ignore your sweaty palms

Don't wipe your hands down your trousers or skirt.

Sip water to aid a dry throat

The best is still water at room temperature; bubbles in sparkling water may make you burp!

You know you're shaking, others don't

Knocking knees and shaking hands are often not noticed, unless you hold an A4 sheet of paper in your hands. There is no need to draw attention to it, but don't try and use a laser pointer unless you can guarantee rock-steady hands, which most of us can't.

Ignore your blush

Blushing with embarrassment is rarely as bad as you think, nor is it noticed as much as you think.

Finally, recent research has found that the emotional state of excitement is very akin to that of nervousness. So choose to be excited about your presentation rather than nervous.

How do I remember what I want to say?

Remembering what you want to say word for word, in the exact order, is a huge ask. Actors do it, with a lot of practice, repetition and rehearsal. For business presentations it is very unlikely that you will be working to a script. However, there are some tips and aides-mémoire to help you remember what you want to say.

Have a structure

If your presentation has a clear structure you will be able to identify key points, words or phrases at the specific structural points. Committing those to memory, rather than the whole presentation, is much easier.

Use triggers

There are some memory techniques that you might find useful. One is to design your presentation and link it to the layout of your own home. You begin at the front door, perhaps by placing a sign on the door with your opening remarks. Then at different stages through your presentation you visualise yourself moving through your home, entering different rooms to move you on to a different section of your talk.

Another technique is to make key words link in a ridiculous way. For instance, you could visualise a large banana with your key word written on the side; as you peel the banana, inside you find your next key word. Then along comes a monkey and takes a bite, which reveals your next section. The monkey has a tag hanging around its neck with your next key word and, finally, the zoo keeper appears wearing an overly large hat upon which is written your closing remarks. Of course you can make up your own ridiculous story; the more outrageous the better, as it's easier for the brain to recall.

Draw or write your own mind map

This is the method I personally use, but I didn't like using mind maps at first; they can take a bit of getting used to. I find handwriting my mind map rather than using software helps to integrate my presentation into my brain. Often I create a mind map to design the presentation, as discussed in **Step 3**. However, I write another mind map the day before I am scheduled to speak. This one has my key points on it and is often placed to the side when I am speaking, but I rarely need to refer to it. Knowing the mind map is there allows me to focus on my audience rather than worrying about whether I will remember what I want to say.

Use crib cards

I started off giving presentations by using crib cards. These were the 6 × 4 index cards, or record cards, which were in regular office use before computers. They are still available and very useful, as the card is sturdy and won't flap or draw as much attention as a sheet of A4 or A5 paper would.

Use of slides

Preparing a slide presentation and thinking you will use that as your memory jogger can be a real disaster. You might have a technology failure and not be able to show your slides. You may end up not being able to see the PC screen, so find yourself turning to view the main screen and thus putting your back to the audience **(one of the presentation don'ts mentioned in Step 6)**. In addition, you are likely to put too much on your slides and fall into the trap of reading them.

If you must, use a slide presentation to jog your memory but not to simply read verbatim.

PowerPoint has a 'notes' view where you can write up your notes against each slide. You can then print out sheets of A4 paper, one per slide, with the slide on the top half and the notes on the bottom. Again, I do not recommend this. There is a tendency to read your notes word for word and you may lose the connection with your audience. Or you might hold the A4 paper in your hand, which is distracting for the audience. It can also provide a false sense of security, persuading you that you don't need to do the next two memory steps. The notes view is useful in the planning process; just don't rely on it as your memory technique.

Record, replay and rehearse

An alternative, and sometimes time-saving, technique is to record one of your presentation practices. You can then replay it while you are cooking the dinner, listen to it while driving or even when exercising in the gym. On the odd occasions where I need to learn a speech word for word, I will record it once straight through, then with deliberate pauses so that I can fill in the blanks when listening to the recording and check whether I remembered correctly. A bit like those audio exercises when learning a foreign language.

Practise, practise, practise

Nothing commits words to memory more than practice, so if you have the time keep rehearsing. Aim to remember the gist; it doesn't have to be word for word.

How do I make a boring subject interesting?

It is important not to convey to an audience that you find your topic uninteresting **(as discussed in Step 4)**. The first place to start with how to make a boring subject interesting is with your own thoughts. If you think your subject is boring . . . it will be!

Why you?

Whether you are speaking about the breeding cycle of fruit flies, the geological structure of the Grand Canyon or the UK tax system, you first need to ask 'why?'. Not why this presentation, but why are *you* giving this presentation.

Where is your expertise, where is your passion in the subject and how can you convey that to your audience?

Look for the WIIFM

Then, to make your subject interesting to the audience and not just to you, you need to take a look at why the audience are hearing your presentation?

Where is their interest? If it is the UK tax system, their interest might not be in the system itself but more in how they could reduce their tax bill. Perhaps the audience for the Grand Canyon presentation are students who need the knowledge for an exam, in which case focus on making the key facts as clear and memorable as possible; or perhaps holidaymakers about to go on a visit who might be most interested in the best viewpoint and café?

In the public speaking profession, this is often referred to as tuning into Channel WIIFM (What's In It For Me?), with 'Me' meaning the audience, not the speaker.

So think about:

- What do they need to know?
- Why do they need to know it?
- What will they do once they know it?

Keep it short and simple

You may be an expert on your subject, but keep it relevant to your audience. Don't give them all the background technical information unless they really need to know it. Don't tell them the life story of your topic, unless they need to know it. Don't overload your presentation with data or explanations.

Keep it short and simple.

Use analogies and alternatives

Find an alternative way of presenting the information – for instance, the final year accounts of an organisation I belonged to were reported by the treasurer. One year, he opened by asking us all a question: if the bank balance was £1,564 and was turned into pound coins, how far would it reach? Our answers ranged from, half way around the world 'to the moon and back', but our engagement was high and the rest of his talk was short, to the point and peppered with humour and off-the-cuff facts. Only at the end did he reveal the correct answer!

Use media

Earlier on I referred to you, the speaker, as being the most important visual aid in a presentation. While this remains true, if you want to keep the interest of your audience then using different types of visual aids in your presentations can be of real benefit. For instance, you can:

- Insert pictures into your slide presentation.
- Embed appropriate video clips, or make your own to illustrate a point.
- Create a sound file – perhaps an endorsement by a colleague or customer.
- Use music to add extra emphasis to points, or at the beginning and end of your presentations.

Do be careful to consider copyright on images, videos and music though. As a professional speaker, I subscribe to the Performing Right Society, which allows me to play music in public. You probably don't need to go this far, but make sure you use media that is in the public domain, or to which you or your organisation owns the copyright.

Include an activity

While there is often a groan when the presenter says 'and now we'll break for a short exercise. . . ', the fact is that activities keep the engagement high. But don't have activities without a reason, and do keep them on topic if you want to keep that engagement.

When introducing the activity, set it up with a reason for people to engage, such as: 'Now I'm sure you've been wondering what this

"There will be six designated yawning breaks during my presentation. Please pace your boredom accordingly."

Source: © Randy Glasbergen, www.glasbergen.com

means for you . . . I'd like to invite you to take 5 minutes to discuss this in pairs or small groups. So, how will implementing XYZ affect you and what questions do you need answering?'

Use humour

If it works for you, and it doesn't work for everyone, the use of humour can create high levels of engagement and make a presentation more interesting. **See Step 5 for more tips on humour.**

If all else fails . . . strip

When I give a talk on networking and it comes to talking about how best to dress for an event, I start to undress. Not completely, sorry to spoil that picture in your imagination, but partially, to make a point about colour coordination, belts, having pockets and looking business-like versus casual. It certainly captures the attention of my audience!

Putting it into action (the mentor toolkit)

How to work with a manager, mentor or colleague to put your new skills into action

How you choose to use this section will depend on your current level of knowledge and skill and the level that you want to attain. Working with a manager, mentor or colleague to develop your presentation skills can be rewarding and motivating for both parties. Your mentor is likely to enjoy seeing you grow and develop your skills, and by working with you they will also develop their own feedback skills and have the satisfaction of passing on some of their expertise. As the mentee, you are likely to feel supported and more secure in the knowledge that you are not alone in the learning process. You have a more experienced person to turn to for information and advice as well as the opportunity to reflect back on relevant steps, skills and challenges in this book as you develop your skills.

The rest of this section is aimed at providing some guidance on how to arrange a mentor–mentee relationship. Regardless of who you choose to work with, I will refer to them here as your mentor for ease.

So where to start? My suggestion is to consider two key questions:

- Where are your skills now? (Current)
- Where do you want them to be? (Desired)

Start by creating your own skills matrix, as this will help you identify where you need to focus. Based on the steps in this book, in the matrix below list the skills that are important to you and that will help you to deliver great presentations. You can also use the pre- and post-self-assessment questionnaires to identify the skills you want to work on. Then rate your current skill level from basic to excellent for each of these, and also your desired level – remember you do not need to be excellent at everything!

Often we mark ourselves unduly harshly or leniently, so you might like to ask a colleague or your mentor to rate your skills as well.

Skills matrix

Mark the matrix with both your current (C) and desired (D) level of skill.

Skill	Basic	Average	Good	Excellent
Opening a presentation				
Involving the audience				
Using visual aids				
Body language				
Vocal variety				
Getting your message across clearly				
Handling questions				
Closing powerfully				
Other. . .				
Other. . .				
Other. . .				
Other. . .				
Other. . .				
Other. . .				

Deciding who to work with

A mentor is usually someone who already has the skills and knowledge you are seeking to acquire, and who is able to provide you with support and guidance. They do not teach you the necessary skills, nor do they do things for you. Rather, they encourage you and provide feedback to help you to pursue your own learning. Can you think of someone like that who could help you with your presentation skills?

A mentoring arrangement should be a relationship that is based on mutual respect and trust. As you will be asking your mentor to provide you with some feedback, it is important that you value their opinions and are willing to listen. The feedback, if it is good quality, won't always be on what you did well, sometimes it will be about how to improve. Choose your mentor wisely and check with them that they are able to provide you with the time and the feedback you need.

It is helpful to have the relationship formalised, and some guidance on this process can be found below. However, some people decide to keep their mentoring relationship informal; the problem here is that the mentor may not know what is wanted or needed from them. In this situation you probably won't gain as much as from a formalised relationship. However, you can have more than one mentor – for instance, you may know one person who is very skilled at getting the audience engaged and someone else who creates clear and elegant PowerPoint presentations.

Ideally your mentor will be available to meet up with you in person and see you give one or more presentations.

A mentor checklist

Your mentor should hopefully satisfy most of the following criteria:

- accessible;
- someone you respect and trust;
- knowledgeable about presentations;
- experienced in making presentations;
- able to provide constructive feedback;
- willing to help and to hold mentoring meetings with you.

How to create the relationship

Once you have identified someone you would like as your mentor, contact the person to explain what you are looking for and to ask them if they will agree to mentor you. You may need to be specific about your needs, so think in advance about what you need help with (refer back to the skills matrix), how you would like them to help you and how often you want to meet.

At your first meeting it is useful to agree the following:

- What do you need?
- What can they offer?
- How much time can they spare?
- When and where will you meet?
- How would you like your feedback? In person, by email, positive first then developmental, or just developmental?
- What support outside the mentoring meetings are they able to give you? For instance, answering email queries, giving guidance on developing your slides, holding practice run-throughs with you, watching one of your presentations.
- How confidential will the meetings be?
- How much feedback will they give to your line manager (assuming they are not the same person)?

Take your completed skills matrix along to your first meeting with your mentor so that you can share it with them. This will help you both to identify what you will work on first.

Between meetings

To develop any skill, and that of giving presentations is no different, practice is required.

In between your mentoring meetings you should aim to work on one or two areas at a time. Don't try to do a fantastic presentation from the outset.

Allow yourself time between meetings to develop your skills; so weekly meetings might be too frequent unless you are giving presentations on a daily basis.

Keep a reflections log

After each presentation, mini-presentation or perhaps meeting where you contributed, complete a reflections log:

- What went well? Why?
- What reaction did you get from the audience?
- What did you try out? How did it go?
- What did you learn?
- What will you do differently next time?

Take these points with you to each mentoring meeting as they can form the basis of discussion.

Use this book as a guide

This book is here to help you develop your skills. Buying it and just keeping it on your shelves and hoping for something magical to happen is a wasted opportunity. You will need to work through the steps and review your progress regularly. You could start at **Step 1** and work your way through, but it may be more appropriate for you to start somewhere else . . . perhaps **Step 9** if confidence is something you want to work on.

Part 2, putting the skills into action, lists areas in which you might be required to give presentations. You could use this list as a guide for seizing opportunities in the workplace.

Part 3 helps you work your way through some common presenting challenges. If you find one of these is your particular nemesis then start here.

Where to present?

Most of all, you will need the opportunity to get on your feet and give presentations. If this is a skill you are not getting the chance to practise in the workplace, but one you want to develop – perhaps to help you secure your next role, or prepare for your next interview – then there are other ways to get on your feet and develop your presentation skills if you are willing to invest a little of your own time.

Many clubs and societies provide opportunities to present, so perhaps joining the committee of one could be your route. Alternatively, join an organisation that specifically encourages the development of presentation skills, such as Toastmasters (**www .toastmasters.org**) or JCI (**www.jciuk.org.uk** or **www.jci.cc**), or a speakers club (**www.the-asc.org.uk**).

Organisations such as these, but especially Toastmasters, provide structured training in presenting to different group sizes on different topics in an enjoyable and supportive environment. You will also get the opportunity to give feedback to other presenters, which is a great way of learning in itself. You might even choose to enter public speaking competitions; scary as that might sound now, it's a great way to develop your confidence.

Finally, think about the guidance in this book when you are in the audience for presentations. Identify what the presenter is doing well; think about where they could improve and what tips you can learn from them.

There are plenty of videos of presentations on the internet. I recommend TED talks (**www.ted.com**) as a source of inspiration and ideas, as well as different presentation styles.

questionnaire

As you read the introduction you were encouraged to take a pre-self-assessment questionnaire to help you assess your skills. Here is the questionnaire again. Having read this book, or part of it, and hopefully put some of the tips into practice, you are invited to retake the questionnaire to help you assess your progress. Remember, Rome wasn't built in a day, neither were presentation skills learned in a day or from simply reading a book. But using the tools, tips and techniques contained in this book will help you develop effective presentations.

Post-assessment

Through completing this questionnaire again you will be able to assess which areas you now enjoy about giving presentations, what now gives you energy and whether you still need to find a way to do certain things more often.

Score yourself on a scale of 1 to 10, with 10 indicating a high level of confidence and skill and 1 the lowest.

1. I feel energised by speaking to people.

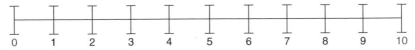

2. I rarely suffer from nerves when speaking in public.

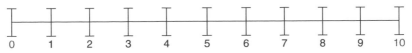

3. I find it easy to express my thoughts.

4. I find it easy to speak up in meetings.

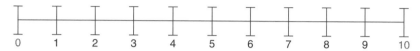

5. I like crafting words to express myself.

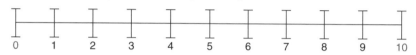

6. I enjoy being the centre of attention.

7. I am confident in my use of PowerPoint.

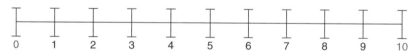

8. I find it easy to make persuasive presentations.

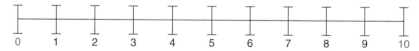

9. I use my body and gestures effectively when communicating to others.

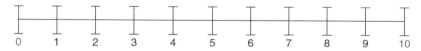

10. I frequently take up opportunities to present to people.

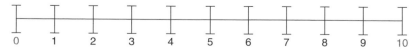

If your score is between 80 and 100 you're now very confident at giving presentations and enjoy the limelight. However, be aware that overconfidence may have crept in and you perhaps could prepare your presentations a little more, rather than 'wing' them.

If your score is between 50 and 80 there is still room to improve your confidence and ability at presenting, but you have learned a fair amount.

If your score is below 50 you are likely to need a confidence boost as well as improved skills. You might like to go back to read **Step 9** on confidence and then return to **Step 1** and work your way through the book. Or use the skills matrix above to guide you.

Keep in mind that this is your opinion; you might like to ask your manager, mentor or colleagues to score you as well.

Good luck and happy presenting.

Kate

What did you think of this book?

We're really keen to hear from you about this book, so that we can make our publishing even better.

Please log on to the following website and leave us your feedback.

It will only take a few minutes and your thoughts are invaluable to us.

www.pearsoned.co.uk/bookfeedback

Bibliography and further reading

Barrell, A., Gill, D. and Rigby, M., 2013. *Show me the Money: how to find the cash to get your business off the ground.* Elliott and Thompson: London.

Buzan, T., 2010. *The Mind Map Book: unlock your creativity, boost your memory, change your life.* BBC Active: London.

Cialdini, R.B., 2009. *Influence: science and practice.* Pearson: Harlow.

Covey, S., 2004. *The Seven Habits of Highly Effective People: powerful lessons in personal change.* Simon & Schuster: London.

Doolan, P., 2015. *Happiness by Design: finding pleasure and purpose in life.* Penguin: London.

Duarte, N., 2008. *slide:ology: the art and science of creating great presentations.* O'Reilly Media: Sebastopol, CA.

Grant, A., 2013. *Give and Take: a revolutionary approach to success.* Weidenfeld & Nicolson: London.

Lencioni, P., 2002. *Five Dysfunctions of a Team: a leadership fable.* Jossey-Bass: San Francisco, CA.

Martin, S., 2008. *Born Standing Up: a comic's life.* Scribner: New York.

Moon, J., 2010. *How to Make an IMPACT: influence, inform and impress with your reports, presentations, business documents, charts and graphs.* Pearson: Harlow.

Parkin, M., 2010. *Tales for Trainers: using stories and metaphors to facilitate learning.* Kogan Page: London.

Reynolds, G., 2011. *Presentation Zen.* New Riders: Berkeley, CA.

Strunk, W. and White, E.B., 1999. *The Elements of Style.* 4th ed. Pearson: New York.

Index